Cool
Chunky
Knits

Cool Chunky Knits

Tabetha Hedrick

STACKPOLE
BOOKS

Lanham   Boulder   New York   London

To my daughters, Ayla and Sophie,
for always being my biggest cheerleaders
and greatest inspiration.

Copyright © 2016 by Tabetha Hedrick

Published by Stackpole Books
An imprint of Globe Pequot
Trade Division of The Rowman & Littlefield Publishing Group, Inc.
4501 Forbes Boulevard, Suite 200, Lanham, Maryland 20706
www.rowman.com

Distributed by National Book Network

Printed in the United States of America

First edition

Cover design by Tessa J. Sweigert
Photography by Tabetha Hedrick

Library of Congress Cataloging-in-Publication Data

Hedrick, Tabetha, author.
    Cool chunky knits : 26 fast & fashionable cowls, shawls, shrugs & more for bulky & super bulky yarns / Tabetha Hedrick. — First edition.
        pages   cm
    Includes index.
    ISBN 978-0-8117-1648-2
    1. Knitting.   2. Dress accessories.   3. Textured yarn.   I. Title.
TT825.H43 2016
746.43'2—dc23
                                                                2015035669

Contents

Acknowledgments

Taking on an entire book is such a massive undertaking and I could not have done it without so many supportive family members and friends. First, my biggest thanks to my husband, Jeremy, for championing my fiber obsession and this book with grace and humor. And to my daughters, Ayla and Sophie, for their patience in my long hours to get it all done. They are my light and stars that guide me in every choice I make.

My most heartfelt gratitude also goes to my mom, Cynthia Spillane, for reminding me to keep reaching, every day, even when I don't think I can.

HUGE thanks to my amazing friends Jill Wright, Corrina Ferguson, Mary Beth Temple, Lindsey Stephens, Charles Voth, Rose Tussing, Justine Chrysler, Amy Alcorn, and all of my Knitting Group Peeps for being not only my models, tech editors, sample knitters, proofreaders, cheerleaders, and sounding boards, but also such wonderful people for putting up with me for so long. You all deserve all the rewards.

I owe so many other kudos to my mentors, colleagues, and friends in the industry for their encouragement, support, and advice, and for those first opportunities that helped me grow to where I am today, especially to Kara Gott Warner, Felicia Lo, Trisha Malcolm, Barb Bettegnies, Susan Mills, Stacey Winklepleck, Susan Gibbs, and Amy Gunderson.

And lastly, I am sincerely thankful to Pam Hoenig, my editor, for encouraging this book-publishing journey. Her support of my creative process and her sweet guidance have been a blessing.

Introduction

Knitters revel in the world of chunky yarn, and why not? Chunky yarn brings glorious instant gratification whether knitting a small accessory or a larger garment. But I started to notice a trend some years ago that all of the chunky yarn knits were super baggy, super bulky, and super—well—reminiscent of mountain-men wear. Not only that, but the pattern options were few, with scarves and hats being the most common choices.

Chunky can be trendy, fun, casual, and beautiful! It can be lightweight enough to wear on those warmer spring days, the cool summer nights, and throughout the fall. It can be cute enough to dress up with heels and casual enough to dress down with jeans. So I decided it was high time to have a collection of knittable, wearable garments and accessories that look great and feel good year-round.

In this book, you'll find small, easy projects such as cowls, scarves, headbands, and bracelets, as well as a great selection of pullovers, shrugs, and vests just perfect for layering (or wearing on their own). You get all of the joy of fast knitting with chunky yarn *and* all of the delights of beautiful texture, stunning color, and delightfully fun projects. Whether a new knitter or advanced one, seeking adventure or relaxation, *Cool Chunky Knits* has the perfect knit for you.

Monday Moebius Cowl

Create luxurious texture and a gentle woven look with slipped stitches. This cowl, with its easy construction and thick yarn, is knit up super quickly, giving you a cowl that wears well for any occasion.

Finished Measurements
Width: 12½"/32 cm
Length: 55¼"/140 cm before seaming

Yarn
Universal Classic Uno, super bulky weight #6 yarn (70% acrylic, 30% wool; 90 yd/5 oz, 82 m/150 g per skein) 3 balls #404 Perfect Blues

Needles and Other Materials
• US size 17 (12.75 mm) knitting needles or size needed to obtain gauge
• Tapestry needle

Finished Gauge
10 sts x 15 rows in Loop St, blocked = 4"/10 cm
Save time by taking time to check gauge.

Note
• This cowl is worked flat in one piece, then seamed.

Stitch Pattern
Loop Stitch (multiple of 2 sts + 2)
Row 1 (RS): Knit.
Row 2 (WS): *K1, sl1 wyib; rep from * to last 2 sts, k2.
Row 3: Knit.
Row 4: K2, *sl1 wyib, k1; rep from * to end.
Rep Rows 1–4 for patt.

Cowl

CO 32 sts.
Work Loop St until cowl measures a finished length
    of approx 55¼"/140 cm long, ending with Row 4.
BO on next RS row.

Finishing

Block to measurements.
Twist the cowl one time, then seam the ends together.
Weave in ends.

Apple River Shrug

Skill Level: **Intermediate**

You'll adore the unique construction of this relaxed, comfortable shrug, as well as how quickly it knits up. The subtle lace pattern works fabulously with the soft self-striping yarn, allowing the final shape to really shine.

Sizes
Woman's XS (S, M, L, XL, 2XL, 3XL)

Finished Measurements
Bust (buttoned): 31 (36, 39½, 43½, 47, 52, 55½)"/78.5
    (91.5, 100.5, 110.5, 119.5, 132, 141) cm
Length (before grafting): 15¼ (16½, 18, 19, 20¼, 21½,
    22¼)"/38.5 (42, 45.5, 48.5, 51.5, 54.5, 56.5) cm

Yarn
Universal Classic Shades Frenzy, chunky weight #5 yarn
    (70% acrylic, 30% wool; 158 yd/3.5 oz, 144 m/100 g
    per skein)
3 (4, 4, 5, 5, 6, 6) skeins #909 Attic Light

Needles and Other Materials
• 24" (60 cm) circular knitting needle, US size 10 (6 mm)
  or size needed to obtain gauge
• 2 stitch holders
• 1"/2.5 cm button
• Tapestry needle

Finished Gauge
15 sts x 21 rows in Wave Lace Patt, blocked = 4"/10 cm
Save time by taking time to check gauge.

Notes
• The shrug is worked in two parts, right and left, before
  being grafted together at the center back using the
  Kitchener stitch (see page 99 for a photo tutorial).
• The border around the shrug is worked when seamed.
• Stitch patterns include selvedge stitches.
• See page 90 for a photo tutorial for cable cast-on.

Stitch Patterns
K1, P1 Rib (multiple of 2 sts +2)
Row 1: K1, *k1, p1; rep from * to last st, k1.
Rep Row 1 for patt.

Wave Lace Pattern (multiple of 9 sts + 2)
Row 1 and all odd-numbered rows (WS): K1, purl to
    last st, k1.
Row 2 (RS): K1, *yo, k7, k2tog; rep from * to last st, k1.
Row 4: K1, *k1, yo, k6, k2tog; rep from * to last st, k1.
Row 6: K1, *k2, yo, k5, k2tog; rep from * to last st, k1.
Row 8: K1, *k3, yo, k4, k2tog; rep from * to last st, k1.
Row 10: K1, *k4, yo, k3, k2tog; rep from * to last st, k1.
Row 12: K1, *k5, yo, k2, k2tog; rep from * to last st, k1.
Row 14: K1, *k6, yo, k1, k2tog; rep from * to last st, k1.
Row 16: K1, *k7, yo, k2tog; rep from * to last st, k1.

Row 18: K1, *ssk, k7, yo; rep from * to last st, k1.
Row 20: K1, *ssk, k6, yo, k1; rep from * to last st, k1.
Row 22: K1, *ssk, k5, yo, k2; rep from * to last st, k1.
Row 24: K1, *ssk, k4, yo, k3; rep from * to last st, k1.
Row 26: K1, *ssk, k3, yo, k4; rep from * to last st, k1.
Row 28: K1, *ssk, k2, yo, k5; rep from * to last st, k1.
Row 30: K1, *ssk, k1, yo, k6; rep from * to last st, k1.
Row 32: K1, *ssk, yo, k7; rep from * to last st, k1.
Rep Rows 1–32 for patt.

Wave Lace Pattern

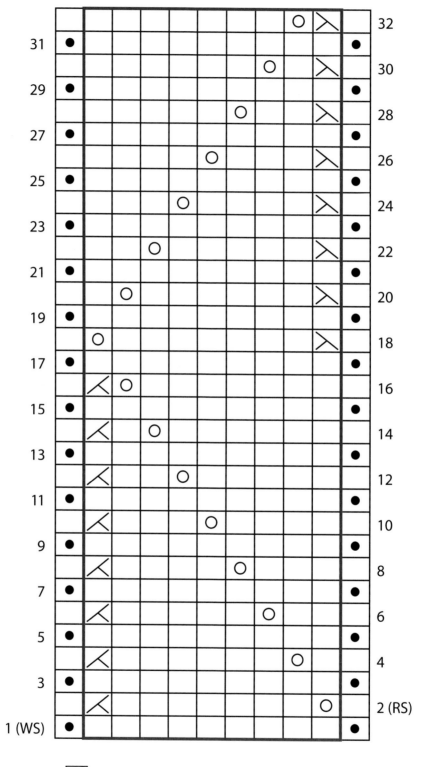

	RS: k; WS: p
●	WS: k
O	yo
⟋	k2tog
⟍	ssk

Finished Measurements

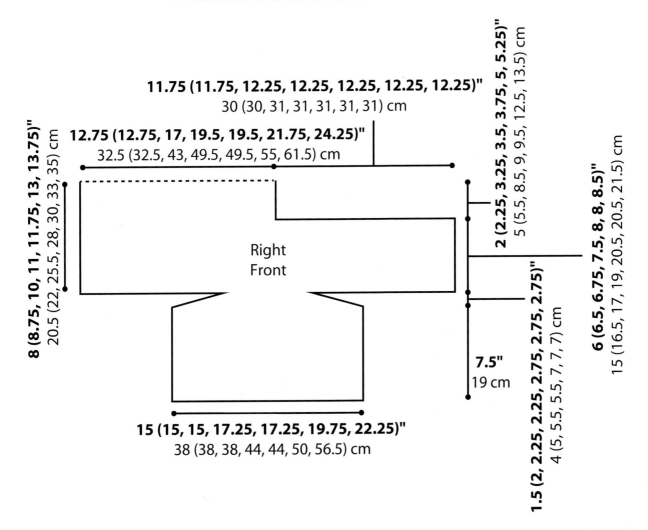

11.75 (11.75, 12.25, 12.25, 12.25, 12.25, 12.25)"
30 (30, 31, 31, 31, 31, 31) cm

12.75 (12.75, 17, 19.5, 19.5, 21.75, 24.25)"
32.5 (32.5, 43, 49.5, 49.5, 55, 61.5) cm

8 (8.75, 10, 11, 11.75, 13, 13.75)"
20.5 (22, 25.5, 28, 30, 33, 35) cm

2 (2.25, 3.25, 3.5, 3.75, 5, 5.25)"
5 (5.5, 8.5, 9, 9.5, 12.5, 13.5) cm

6 (6.5, 6.75, 7.5, 8, 8, 8.5)"
15 (16.5, 17, 19, 20.5, 20.5, 21.5) cm

1.5 (2, 2.25, 2.25, 2.75, 2.75, 2.75)"
4 (5, 5.5, 5.5, 7, 7, 7) cm

Right
Front

7.5"
19 cm

15 (15, 15, 17.25, 17.25, 19.75, 22.25)"
38 (38, 38, 44, 44, 50, 56.5) cm

Right Sleeve

CO 56 (56, 56, 65, 65, 74, 83) sts.
Work K1, P1 Rib for 11 rows, ending with a RS row.
Next row (WS): Change to Wave Lace Patt and work even
   until sleeve measures a finished length of 7½"/19 cm
   from cast-on edge, ending with a WS row.

Shape Sleeve Cap
*NOTE: If there are not enough sts to work a yo-decrease
combination, work them as St st.*
BO 3 (2, 2, 2, 2, 2, 3) sts at beg of next 4 (2, 10, 4, 10, 2,
   10) rows, then 4 (3, 3, 3, 3, 3, 4) sts at beg of the foll
   4 (8, 2, 8, 4, 12, 4) rows—28 (28, 30, 33, 33, 34, 37)
   sts rem.

Right Body

Row 1 (RS): Using cable cast-on, CO 32 (32, 40, 43, 43,
   47, 50) sts at beg of row, work even in est patt to end—
   60 (60, 70, 76, 76, 81, 87) sts.
Row 2 (WS): Using cable cast-on, CO 32 (32, 40, 43, 43,
   47, 50) sts at beg of row, work even in est patt to end—
   92 (92, 110, 119, 119, 128, 137) sts.
Work even in est patt until right body measures a finished
   length of 6 (6½, 6¾, 7½, 8, 8, 8½)"/15 (16.5, 17, 19,
   20.5, 20.5, 21.5) cm from first cable cast-on row, ending with a WS row.
Next row (RS): BO 44 (44, 46, 46, 46, 46, 46) sts at beg
   of row, work even to end of row—48 (48, 64, 73, 73,
   82, 91) sts.
Continue in est patt until right body measures a finished
   length of 8 (8¾, 10, 11, 11¾, 13, 13¾)"/20.5 (22, 25.5,
   28, 30, 33, 35) cm from second cable cast-on row, ending with a WS row.
Place stitches on stitch holder.

Left Sleeve

Work as for Right Sleeve to Right Body.

Left Body

Row 1 (RS): Using cable cast-on, CO 32 (32, 40, 43, 43, 47, 50) sts at beg of row, work even in est patt to end—60 (60, 70, 76, 76, 81, 87) sts.

Row 2 (WS): Using cable cast-on, CO 32 (32, 40, 43, 43, 47, 50) sts at beg of row, work even in est patt to end—92 (92, 110, 119, 119, 128, 137) sts.

Work even in est patt until left body measures a finished length of 6 (6½, 6¾, 7½, 8, 8, 8½)"/15 (16.5, 17, 19, 20.5, 20.5, 21.5) cm from cable cast-on row, ending with a RS row.

Next row (WS): BO 44 (44, 46, 46, 46, 46, 46) sts at beg of row, work even to end of row—48 (48, 64, 73, 73, 82, 91) sts.

Continue in est patt until left body measures a finished length of 8 (8¾, 10, 11, 11¾, 13, 13¾)"/20.5 (22, 25.5, 28, 30, 33, 35) cm from first cable cast-on row, ending with a WS row. Place stitches on stitch holder.

Finishing

Block to schematic measurements.

Using Kitchener stitch, graft back panels together.

With tapestry needle, sew angled part at top of sleeves to body.

Fold shrug in half at shoulders and sew side seams.

Fold sleeves in half and sew sleeve seam from underarm to cuff.

Lower Edging

With RS facing, beg at lower edge of right front and pick up and knit 110 (121, 131, 147, 157, 167, 175) sts evenly across entire bottom edge of shrug.

Row 1 (WS): *K1, p1; rep from * to last st, k1.

Row 2 (RS): K2, *p1, k1; rep from * to last st, k1.

Rep Rows 1–2 until band measures 2"/5 cm.

BO loosely.

Front Edging

With RS facing, beg at lower edge of right front edging and pick up and knit 109 (111, 123, 125, 127, 137, 139) sts evenly around right front, back neck, and left front.

Row 1 (WS): *Sl1, p1; rep from * to last st, k1.

Row 2 (RS): Sl1, k1, *p1, k1; rep from * to last st, k1.

Rep Rows 1–2.

Rep Row 1.

Buttonhole row (RS): Work 8 sts in est patt, yo, k2tog, continue in est patt to end.

Repeat Rows 1–2 until band measures 2"/5 cm.

BO loosely in patt.

Sew button onto left front edging to correspond to buttonhole.

Weave in ends.

Hanalei Wrap

Skill Level: Intermediate

When using a bulky weight yarn, leaf lace becomes all the more stunning. This rectangular wrap is no exception! Long, warm, and deliciously cozy, you'll love knitting it from start to finish.

Arrowhead Lace

10	●	●	●													●	●	●	
			●					○	⋀	○						●			9
8	●	●	●													●	●	●	
			●				○		⋀		○					●			7
6	●	●	●													●	●	●	
			●			○			⋀			○				●			5
4	●	●	●													●	●	●	
			●		○				⋀				○			●			3
2 (WS)	●	●	●													●	●	●	
			●	○					⋀					○		●			1 (RS)

□ RS: k; WS: p
● RS: p; WS: k
○ yo
⋀ s2kp

Finished Measurements

Width: 16¼"/41.5 cm
Length: 62"/157.5 cm

Yarn

Wisdom Yarns Poems Chunky, super bulky weight #6 yarn
(100% wool; 110 yd/3.5 oz, 100 m/100 g per skein)
4 balls #903 Autumn Haze

Needles and Other Materials

• 24" (60 cm) circular knitting needle, US size 13 (9 mm)
  or size needed to obtain gauge
• Tapestry needle

Finished Gauge

13 sts x 15 rows in Arrowhead Lace, blocked = 4"/10 cm
Save time by taking time to check gauge.

Note

• This shawl is worked flat from side to side.

Special Stitch

s2kp: Slip 2 sts together knitwise, knit 1, then pass both
slipped sts over together; for a photo tutorial, see
page 94.

Stitch Pattern

Arrowhead Lace (multiple of 12 sts + 5)

Row 1 (RS): K2, *p1, yo, k4, s2kp, k4, yo; rep from * to last 3 sts, p1, k2.

Rows 2, 4, 6, 8, and 10 (WS): K3, *p11, k1; rep from * to last 2 sts, k2.

Row 3: K2, *p1, k1, yo, k3, s2kp, k3, yo, k1; rep from * to last 3 sts, p1, k2.

Row 5: K2, *p1, k2, yo, k2, s2kp, k2, yo, k2; rep from * to last 3 sts, p1, k2.

Row 7: K2, *p1, k3, yo, k1, s2kp, k1, yo, k3; rep from * to last 3 sts, p1, k2.

Row 9: K2, *p1, k4, yo, s2kp, yo, k4; rep from * to last 3 sts, p1, k2.

Rep Rows 1–10 for patt.

Wrap

CO 53 sts.

Set-up row (WS): K3, *p11, k1; rep from * to last 2 sts, k2.

Begin Arrowhead Lace patt and work even until shawl measures a finished length of approx 62"/157.5 cm from cast-on edge, ending with a RS row.

BO loosely.

Finishing

Weave in ends.

Block to measurements.

Ashaway Scarf

Skill Level: Easy

Linen stitch is rich with texture, allowing the bold colors of this scarf to pop! You'll love how surprisingly easy this pattern is, but not as much as you'll love dressing up the finished scarf.

Finished Measurements

Width: 4¼"/10.5 cm
Length: 80"/203 cm

Yarn

Universal Classic Shades Big Time,
    super bulky weight #6 yarn (70%
    acrylic, 30% wool; 85 yd/5 oz, 77
    m/150 g per skein)
    2 balls #804 Grapevine

Needles and Other Materials

- US size 17 (12.75 mm) knitting
  needles or size needed to obtain
  gauge
- US size N/P-15 (10 mm) or P/Q
  (15 mm) crochet hook
- Tapestry needle

Finished Gauge

11 sts x 18 rows in Linen St, blocked
    = 4"/10 cm
*Save time by taking time to check
    gauge.*

Note

- This scarf is worked flat in one
  piece. The decorative fringe is
  added separately.

Close-up of the Linen Stitch.

Stitch Pattern

Linen Stitch (multiple of 2 sts + 2)

Row 1 (RS): Sl1 wyib, *k1, sl1 wyif; rep from * to last
    st, k1.
Row 2 (WS): Sl1 wyib, *p1, sl1 wyib; rep from * to last
    st, k1.
Rep Rows 1–2 for patt.

Scarf

CO 12 sts.
Work Linen St until scarf measures approx 80"/203 cm
    long, ending with a RS row.
BO loosely in pattern.

Finishing

Block to measurements. Weave in ends.

Fringe

Cut 12 pieces of yarn 16"/40.5 cm long. Fold one strand in half and grasp it at the fold. Starting with RS facing, at corner of scarf on selvedge edge, insert crochet hook from back to front. Place yarn fold (the loop) over the hook and pull it through to back of scarf. Wrap the two tails of the yarn around the hook and pull through the loop that is on the hook, being sure to pull tightly. One fringe has been added. Continue to add fringe evenly approx every 2 sts all the way to corner. Repeat on other end of scarf.

Marias Cowl

Skill Level: **Intermediate**

Long and loose, this cowl features easy diagonal cables that are as fun to knit as they look in the final project. Dress up any outfit with a chic casual effect by wearing it down or double it up for cozy comfort.

Finished Measurements
Width: 6"/15 cm
Length: 67"/170 cm before seaming

Yarn
Premier Yarns Deborah Norville Saturate, bulky weight
   #5 yarn (84% acrylic, 16% polyamide; 92 yd/1.75 oz,
   84 m/50 g per skein)
   3 balls #455-01 Granite

Needles and Other Materials
• US size 11 (8 mm) knitting needles or size needed
   to obtain gauge
• Cable needle
• Tapestry needle

Finished Gauge
15 sts x 16 rows in Diagonal Cable patt, blocked
   = 4"/10 cm
Save time by taking time to check gauge.

Note
• This cowl is worked flat in one piece, then seamed.

Special Stitches
1/1 RPC: Slip 1 st to cable needle and hold in back, p1,
   k1 from cable needle.
2/1 RPC: Slip 1 st to cable needle and hold in back, k2,
   p1 from cable needle.
1/1 RC: Slip 1 st to cable needle and hold in back, k1,
   k1 from cable needle.

Stitch Pattern
Diagonal Cable (multiple of 21 sts + 2)
Row 1 (RS): Sl1, p1, [p1, 2/1 RPC] 4 times, p4, k1.
Row 2 (WS): Sl1 wyif, k5, [p2, k2] 4 times, k1.
Row 3: Sl1, [p1, 2/1 RPC] 4 times, p4, k2.
Row 4: Sl1 wyif, p1, k5, [p2, k2] 4 times.
Row 5: Sl1, [2/1 RPC, p1] 4 times, p3, 1/1 RC, k1.
Row 6: Sl1 wyif, p2, k3, [k2, p2] 4 times, k1.
Row 7: Sl1, 1/1 RPC, [p1, 2/1 RPC] 3 times, p4, 2/1 RPC, k1.
Row 8: Sl1 wyif, k1, p2, k5, [p2, k2] 3 times, p1, k1.
Row 9: Sl1, p1, [p1, 2/1 RPC] 3 times, p4, 2/1 RPC, p1, k1.
Row 10: Sl1 wyif, k2, p2, k5, [p2, k2] 3 times, k1.
Row 11: Sl1, [p1, 2/1 RPC] 3 times, p4, 2/1 RPC, p1, k2.
Row 12: Sl1 wyif, p1, k2, p2, k5, [p2, k2] 3 times.
Row 13: Sl1, [2/1 RPC, p1] 3 times, p3, 2/1 RPC, p1, 1/1
   RC, k1.
Row 14: Sl1 wyif, [p2, k2] twice, k1, [k2, p2] 3 times, k1.

Diagonal Cable

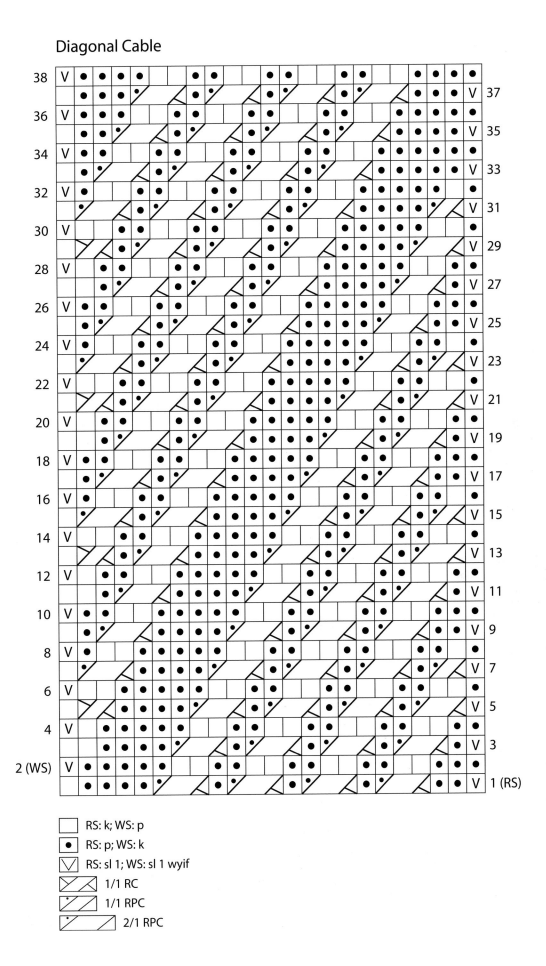

RS: k; WS: p

• RS: p; WS: k

V RS: sl 1; WS: sl 1 wyif

1/1 RC

1/1 RPC

2/1 RPC

Row 15: Sl1, 1/1 RPC, [p1, 2/1 RPC] twice, p4, 2/1 RPC, p1, 2/1 RPC, k1.
Row 16: Sl1 wyif, k1, [p2, k2] twice, k3, [p2, k2] twice, p1, k1.
Row 17: Sl1, p1, [p1, 2/1 RPC] twice, p4, [2/1 RPC, p1] twice, k1.
Row 18: Sl1 wyif, [k2, (p2, k2) twice, k1] twice.
Row 19: Sl1, [p1, 2/1 RPC] twice, p4, [2/1 RPC, p1] twice, k2.
Row 20: Sl1 wyif, p1, [k2, p2] twice, k5, [p2, k2] twice.
Row 21: Sl1, 2/1 RPC, p1, 2/1 RPC, p4, [2/1 RPC, p1] twice, 1/1 RC, k1.
Row 22: Sl1 wyif, [p2, k2] 3 times, k1, [k2, p2] twice, k1.
Row 23: Sl1, 1/1 RPC, p1, 2/1 RPC, p3, [p1, 2/1 RPC] 3 times, k1.
Row 24: Sl1 wyif, k1, [p2, k2] 3 times, k3, p2, k2, p1, k1.
Row 25: Sl1, p2, 2/1 RPC, p4, [2/1 RPC, p1] 3 times, k1.
Row 26: Sl1 wyif, [k2, p2] twice, [k2, p2, k3] twice.
Row 27: Sl1, p1, 2/1 RPC, p4, 2/1 RPC, [k1, 2/1 RPC] twice, p1, k2.
Row 28: Sl1 wyif, p1, [k2, p2] 3 times, k5, p2, k2.
Row 29: Sl1, 2/1 RPC, p4, [2/1 RPC, p1] 3 times, 1/1 RC, k1.
Row 30: Sl1 wyif, [p2, k2] 4 times, k3, p2, k1.
Row 31: Sl1, 1/1 RPC, p3, [p1, 2/1 RPC] 4 times, k1.
Row 32: Sl1 wyif, k1, [p2, k2] 4 times, k3, p1, k1.
Row 33: Sl1, p5, [2/1 RPC, p1] 4 times, k1.
Row 34: Sl1 wyif, [k2, p2] 4 times, k6.
Row 35: Sl1, p4, [2/1 RPC, p1] 4 times, p1, k1.
Row 36: Sl1 wyif, k1, [k2, p2] 4 times, k5.
Row 37: Sl1, p3, [2/1 RPC, p1] 4 times, p2, k1.
Row 38: Sl1 wyif, k4, [p2, k2] 4 times, k2.
Rep Rows 1–38 for patt.

Cowl

CO 23 sts.
Set-up row: Sl1 wyif, k4, [p2, k2] 4 times, k2.
Work Diagonal Cable patt until cowl measures a finished length of approx 67"/144.5 cm long, ending with Row 38.
BO on next RS row.

Finishing

Block to measurements.
Seam the ends together.
Weave in ends.

Kachess Hat

Skill Level: Easy

Kachess Hat is a down-to-earth pattern with the quiet, simple grace of beautiful ribbing. Perfect for warming up on a late winter day, this hat is a snap to knit up for the whole family!

Sizes
Adult S (L)

Finished Measurements
Circumference: 18½ (20½)"/47 (52) cm
Length to crown: 10"/25.5 cm

Yarn
Lion Brand Jiffy, bulky weight #5 yarn (100% acrylic;
    135 yd/3 oz, 105 m/85 g per skein)
    1 ball #450-134 Avocado

Needles and Other Materials
• 16" (40 cm) circular knitting needle, US size 10 (6 mm)
  or size needed to obtain gauge
• US size 10 (6 mm) set of 4 double-pointed needles or
  size needed to obtain gauge
• Tapestry needle

Finished Gauge
14 sts x 20 rows in Textured Rib, blocked = 4"/10 cm
Save time by taking time to check gauge.

Stitch Patterns
K1, P1 Pattern (multiple of 2 sts)
Rnd 1: *K1, p1; rep from * to end of rnd.
Rep Rnd 1 for patt.

Textured Rib (multiple of 4 sts)
Rnd 1: *K1, p3; rep from * to end of rnd.
Rep Rnd 1 for patt.

Hat

CO 64 (72) sts. Place marker and join for working in
the round.

Work K1, P1 Patt for a total of 7 rnds.

Increase rnd: *Work in K1, P1 Patt for 16 (18) sts, M1;
rep from * to end of rnd—68 (76) sts.

Change to Textured Rib patt and work even until hat
measures a finished length of approx 9"/23 cm from
cast-on edge.

Crown Shaping

Rnd 1: *K1, p1, p2tog; rep from * to end of rnd—51
(57) sts rem.

Rnd 2: *K1, p2tog; rep from * to end of rnd—34 (38)
sts rem.

Rnd 3: [P2tog] to end of rnd—17 (19) sts rem.

Rnd 4: [P2tog] 8 (9) times, k1—9 (10) sts rem.

Cut 8"/20.5 cm tail, draw through rem stitches, and
pull tight.

Finishing

Weave in ends.
Block to measurements.
Fold brim as desired.

Abita Pullover

Skill Level: Intermediate

Deliciously easy to knit, with a fun diagonal lace, Abita Pullover is all about chic, comfortable style with endless layering possibilities throughout the year.

Sizes

Woman's XS (S, M, L, XL, 2XL, 3XL)

Finished Measurements

Bust circumference (seamed): 31¾ (35¾, 40¼, 43¾, 47¾,
 51¾, 56¼)"/80.5 (91, 102, 111, 121.5, 131.5, 143) cm
Length: 23½ (23½, 24¼, 24¼, 26½, 27¼, 29½)"/59.5
 (59.5, 61.5, 61.5, 67.5, 69, 75) cm

Yarn

Universal Deluxe Chunky, bulky weight #5 yarn (100%
 wool; 120 yd/3.5 oz, 110 m/100 g per skein)
 4 (4, 5, 6, 7, 7, 8) skeins #22271 Heliotrope

Needles and Other Materials

• US size 11 (8 mm) knitting needles or size needed to
 obtain gauge
• 24" (60 cm) circular knitting needle, US size 11 (8 mm)
 or size needed to obtain gauge
• 4 stitch markers
• Tapestry needle

Finished Gauge

11 sts x 17 rows in Diagonal Lace patt, blocked = 4"/10 cm
12 sts x 17 rows in St st, blocked = 4"/10 cm
Save time by taking time to check gauge.

Notes

• This pullover is worked flat in two pieces from cuff to
 cuff. The front and back pieces are then seamed together
 at the sides and top of sleeves.
• Stitch patterns include selvedge stitches.
• See page 90 for photo tutorial for cable cast-on.
• When working sections in stockinette stitch, slip the first
 stitch of each row.

Stitch Patterns

Diagonal Lace (multiple of 6 sts + 2)

Row 1 (RS): K1, *(k2tog, yo) twice, k2; rep from * to last
 st, k1.
Row 2 and all even-numbered rows (WS): K1, purl across
 to last st, k1.
Row 3: K1, *k1, (k2tog, yo) twice, k1; rep from * to last
 st, k1.

Diagonal Lace

□ RS: k; WS: p

▣ WS: k

◻ yo

⊿ k2tog

Row 5: K1, *k2, (k2tog, yo) twice; rep from * to last st, k1.

Row 7: K3, *k1, (k2tog, yo) twice, k1; rep from * to last 5 sts, k1, k2tog, yo, k2.

Row 9: K1, k2tog, yo, *k2, (k2tog, yo) twice; rep from * to last 5 sts, k2, k2tog, yo, k1.

Row 11: K2, k2tog, yo, *k2, (k2tog, yo) twice; rep from * to last 4 sts, k4.

Rep Rows 1–12 for patt.

Stockinette Stitch (St st)

Row 1 (RS): Sl1, knit to end.

Row 2 (WS): Sl1, purl to last st, k1.

Rep Rows 1–2 for patt.

Back

Right Sleeve (first sleeve)

CO 20 (20, 20, 20, 26, 26, 32) sts.

Set-up row (WS): K1, purl to last st, k1. Begin Diagonal Lace patt and work even until sleeve measures a finished length of 7 (7½, 8, 8½, 9, 9½, 10)"/18 (19, 20.5, 21.5, 23, 24, 25.5) cm, ending with a WS row.

Next row (RS): Work in patt to last st, place marker (m), k1.

Begin Back Body

Next row (WS): Use the cable cast-on and CO 49 (49, 51, 51, 51, 53, 53) sts at beg of row, k1, purl to m, work in est patt to end of row—69 (69, 71, 71, 77, 79, 85) sts.

Maintaining Diagonal Lace patt before the marker and St st for the body after the m, work even until right sleeve and back measure 9¾ (10¾, 12¼, 13¼, 14¼, 15¼, 16½)"/25 (27.5, 31, 33.5, 36, 38.5, 42) cm from cast-on edge, ending with a WS row.

Finished Measurements

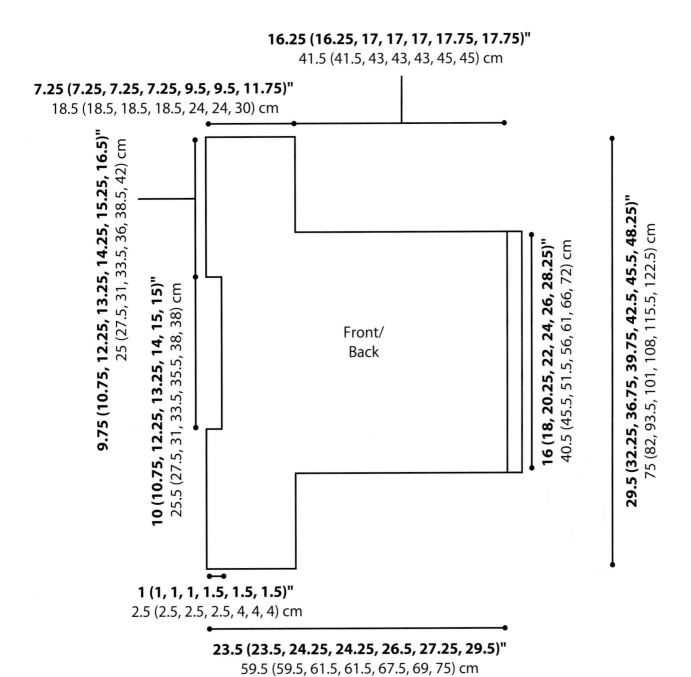

16.25 (16.25, 17, 17, 17, 17.75, 17.75)"
41.5 (41.5, 43, 43, 43, 45, 45) cm

7.25 (7.25, 7.25, 7.25, 9.5, 9.5, 11.75)"
18.5 (18.5, 18.5, 18.5, 24, 24, 30) cm

9.75 (10.75, 12.25, 13.25, 14.25, 15.25, 16.5)"
25 (27.5, 31, 33.5, 36, 38.5, 42) cm

10 (10.75, 12.25, 13.25, 14, 15, 15)"
25.5 (27.5, 31, 33.5, 35.5, 38, 38) cm

Front/
Back

16 (18, 20.25, 22, 24, 26, 28.25)"
40.5 (45.5, 51.5, 56, 61, 66, 72) cm

29.5 (32.25, 36.75, 39.75, 42.5, 45.5, 48.25)"
75 (82, 93.5, 101, 108, 115.5, 122.5) cm

1 (1, 1, 1, 1.5, 1.5, 1.5)"
2.5 (2.5, 2.5, 2.5, 4, 4, 4) cm

23.5 (23.5, 24.25, 24.25, 26.5, 27.25, 29.5)"
59.5 (59.5, 61.5, 61.5, 67.5, 69, 75) cm

Shape Neck

If there are not enough sts to work a yo-k2tog combination, work them as St st.

BO 3 (3, 3, 3, 4, 4, 4) sts at beg of next RS row. Work even in est patt, Diagonal Lace patt for yoke and St st for body, until neck measures a finished length of 10 (10¾, 12¼, 13¼, 14, 15, 15)"/25.5 (27.5, 31, 33.5, 35.5, 38, 38) cm from initial bind-off edge, ending with a WS row.

Next row (RS): Using cable cast-on, CO 3 (3, 3, 3, 4, 4, 4) sts at beg of row. Work even in patt to end of row—69 (69, 71, 71, 77, 79, 85) sts.

Maintain est patt until body measures a finished length of 16 (18, 20¼, 22, 24, 26, 28¼)"/40.5 (45.5, 51.5, 56, 61, 66, 72) cm from initial cast-on edge, ending with a RS row.

Left Sleeve (second sleeve)

Next row (WS): BO 49 (49, 51, 51, 51, 53, 53) sts at beg of row, k1, remove m, work in Diagonal Lace patt to end of row. Maintain est lace patt until sleeve measures a finished length of 7 (7½, 8, 8½, 9, 9½, 10)"/18 (19, 20.5, 21.5, 23, 24, 25.5) cm from body bind-off row, ending with a RS row.

BO loosely on next WS row.

Back Hem

With RS facing, pick up and knit 52 (56, 64, 72, 76, 84, 92) sts evenly across hem of back body.

Row 1 (WS): Sl1, p2, *k2, p2; rep from * to last st, p1.

Row 2 (RS): Sl1, k2, *p2, k2; rep from * to last st, k1.

Rep Rows 1 and 2 until border measures 2½"/6.5 cm, ending with a RS row.

BO on next WS row.

Note that the front and back hems are left open and that the back hem is 1"/2.5 cm longer than the front.

Front

Work as for Back to Back Hem. However, the first sleeve will now be the Left Sleeve on the Front; the second sleeve will now be the Right Sleeve on the Front.

Front Hem

With RS facing, pick up and knit 52 (56, 64, 72, 76, 84, 92) sts evenly across hem of front body.

Row 1 (WS): Sl1, p2, *k2, p2; rep from * to last st, p1.

Row 2 (RS): Sl1, k2, *p2, k2; rep from * to last st, k1.

Rep Rows 1 and 2 until border measures 1½"/4 cm, ending with a RS row.

BO on next WS row.

Finishing

Block to measurements.

Sew top of sleeves from cuff to neck. Sew bottom underarm of sleeves. Sew side seams from armhole to top of ribbing, leaving the sides of the ribbing open.

Neck Ribbing

With RS facing, pick up and knit 80 (88, 96, 104, 112, 120, 120) sts evenly around neck edge. Place marker and join for working in the round.

Rnd 1: *K2, p2; rep from * to end of rnd.

Rep Rnd 1 until neck ribbing measures 1"/2.5 cm.

BO loosely.

Weave in ends.

Fresno Braided Headband

Skill Level: **Easy**

Make use of that leftover yarn from other projects by whipping up a quick headband in less than two hours! Braided I-cords highlight those color-shifting yarns perfectly, promising a stylish accessory for managing hair.

Finished Measurements
Adjustable to head circumference

Yarn
Universal Yarns Poems Chunky, bulky weight #5 yarn
    (100% wool; 110 yd/3.5 oz, 100 m/100 g per skein)
    Approx 25 yd/22 m of #901 Embers

Needles and Other Materials
• US size 11 (8 mm) set of 2 double-pointed needles
• Tapestry needle

Special Stitch
I-cord: See page 96 for a photo tutorial.

Headband

Leaving a 20"/51 cm tail, CO 4 sts.
Work I-cord to 16"/40.5 cm or to desired length.
Cut yarn, leaving a 20"/51 cm tail.
Rep to make 3 I-cords.

Finishing

Knot the ends of the 3 I-cords together. Braid the I-cords.
    Knot together to secure the other end.
Trim the tail ends, as desired, but leave long enough to
    tie the headband together around the head.

Sekiu Hat

Thick, luscious cables unite perfectly with simple ribbing details for a hat that is charming, cozy, and entertaining to knit. Sekiu Hat will easily be one of your favorite projects!

Sizes
Adult S (L)

Finished Measurements
Circumference: 18¼ (21½)"/46.5 (54.5) cm
Length to crown: 8¼ (9)"/21 (23) cm

Yarn
Patons Classic Wool Bulky, bulky weight #5 yarn (100%
    wool; 78 yd/3.5 oz, 71 m/100 g per ball)
    2 balls #9310 Aster Purple

Needles and Other Materials
• 16" (40 cm) circular knitting needle, US size 11 (8 mm)
   or size needed to obtain gauge
• US size 11 (8 mm) set of 4 double-pointed needles or
   size needed to obtain gauge
• Cable needle
• Stitch marker
• Tapestry needle

Finished Gauge
13 sts x 17 rnds in Cable Rib patt, blocked = 4"/10 cm
Save time by taking time to check gauge.

Note
• Hat is worked from the brim to the crown. Start with
   the circular needle and switch to dpns when necessary.

Special Stitches
1/1 RC: Slip 1 st to cable needle and hold in back, k1, k1
    from cable needle.
1/1 LC: Slip 1 st to cable needle and hold in front, k1, k1
    from cable needle.

Stitch Pattern
Cable Rib (multiple of 10 sts)
Rnd 1: *K2, p2, k4, p2; rep from * to end of rnd.
Rnd 2: *K2, p2, 1/1 RC, 1/1 LC, p2; rep from * to end
    of rnd.
Rnd 3: *K2, p2, k4, p2; rep from * to end of rnd.
Rnd 4: *K2, p2, 1/1 LC, 1/1 RC, p2; rep from * to end
    of rnd.
Rep Rnds 1–4 for patt.

Hat

Using circular needle, CO 60 (70) sts. Place marker and join
for working in the round.
Work Cable Rib patt until hat measures 6 (6¾)"/15.5 (17.5)
cm from cast-on edge.

Crown Shaping

Rnd 1: [K2, p2, ssk, k2tog, p2] 6 (7) times—48 (56) sts.
Rnd 2 and all even-numbered rnds: Knit each knit and
purl each purl.
Rnd 3: [K2, p2tog] 12 (14) times—36 (42) sts.
Rnd 5: [K2tog, p1] 12 (14) times—24 (28) sts.
Rnd 7: [K2tog] 12 (14) times—12 (14) sts.
Rnd 9: [K2tog] 6 (7) times—6 (7) sts.
Rnd 10: Knit.
Cut 8"/20.5 cm tail, draw through remaining sts, and
pull tight.

Finishing

Weave in ends.
Block to measurements, as desired.

Calumet Shawlette

Skill Level: Intermediate

Simple lace and soft texture accentuate the delicate beauty of this triangular shawlette. The easy-to-memorize pattern enchants from beginning to end.

Finished Measurements

Wingspan: 54"/137 cm
Depth: 25½"/65 cm

Yarn

Bernat Alpaca, bulky weight #5 yarn (70% acrylic, 30% alpaca; 102 yd/3.5 oz, 93 m/100 g per skein)
2 balls #3007 Natural

Needles and Other Materials

• 32" (80 cm) circular knitting needle, US size 10 (6 mm) or size needed to obtain gauge
• Cable needle
• Tapestry needle

Finished Gauge

12 sts x 20 rows in Lace patt, blocked = 4"/10 cm
Save time by taking time to check gauge.

Note

• Shawl is worked flat, beginning at back of neck.

Garter Tab Cast-On

CO 3 sts.
Rows 1–6: Knit.
Turn tab 90 degrees clockwise and pick up 3 sts along side edge.
Turn tab 90 degrees clockwise again and pick up 3 sts from cast-on edge—9 sts.
Set-up row: Sl1, k3, pm, p1, pm, k4.

Shawl Set-Up

Work the 6-row Set-Up Chart (written instructions below) once—21 sts.
Row 1 (RS): Sl1, k2, yo, p1, yo, sm, k1, sm, yo, p1, yo, k3.
Row 2 (WS): Sl1, k2, p1, k1, p1, sm, p1, sm, p1, k1, p1, k3.
Row 3: Sl1, k2, yo, k1, p1, k1, yo, sm, k1, sm, yo, k1, p1, k1, yo, k3.
Row 4: Sl1, k3, [p1, k1] twice, sm, p1, sm, [k1, p1] twice, k4.
Row 5: Sl1, k2, yo, p1, yo, k3tog, yo, p1, yo, sm, k1, sm, yo, p1, yo, k3tog, yo, p1, yo, k3.
Row 6: Sl1, k4, [p1, k1] twice, k1, sm, p1, sm, k1, [k1, p1] twice, k5.

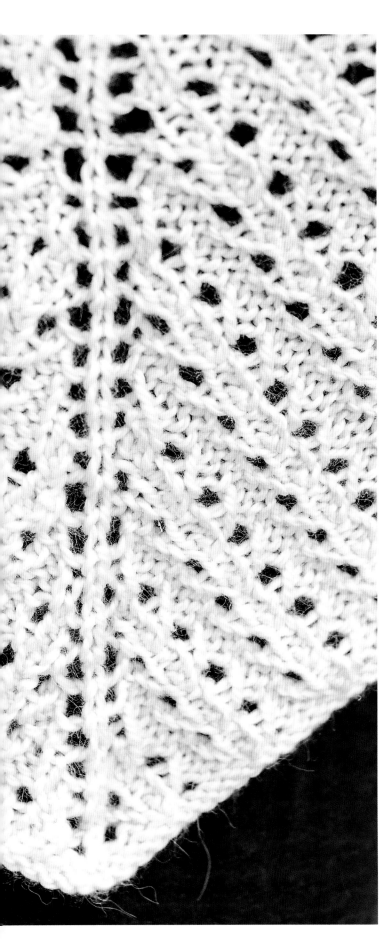

Shawl Body

Rep 20-row Lace Chart (written instructions below) until
shawl measures a depth of 25½"/65 cm or to desired
depth, ending with a RS row.

BO loosely on next WS row.

Row 1 (RS): Sl1, k2, yo, p2, *k1, p1, k1, p2; rep from * to
m, yo, sm, k1, sm, yo, **p2, k1, p1, k1; rep from ** to
last 5 sts, p2, yo, k3.

Row 2 (WS): Sl1, k2, p1, k2, *p1, k1, p1, k2; rep from * to
1 st before m, p1, sm, p1, sm, p1, **k2, p1, k1, p1; rep
from ** to last 6 sts, k2, p1, k3.

Row 3: Sl1, k2, yo, k1, p2, *yo, k3tog, yo, p2; rep from
* to 1 st before m, k1, yo, sm, k1, sm, yo, k1, **p2, yo,
k3tog, yo; rep from ** to last 6 sts, p2, k1, yo, k3.

Row 4: Sl1, k3, p1, k2, *p1, k1, p1, k2; rep from * to 2 sts
before m, p1, k1, sm, p1, sm, k1, p1, **k2, p1, k1, p1;
rep from ** to last 7 sts, k2, p1, k4.

Row 5: Sl1, k2, yo, p1, k1, p2, *k1, p1, k1, p2; rep from
* to 2 sts before m, k1, p1, yo, sm, k1, sm, yo, p1, k1,
**p2, k1, p1, k1; rep from ** to last 7 sts, p2, k1, p1,
yo, k3.

Row 6: Sl1, k2, p1, k1, p1, k2, *p1, k1, p1, k2; rep from
* to 3 sts before m, p1, k1, p1, sm, p1, sm, p1, k1, p1,
** k2, p1, k1, p1; rep from ** to last 8 sts, k2, p1, k1,
p1, k3.

Row 7: Sl1, k2, yo, k1, k2tog, yo, p2, *yo, k3tog, yo, p2;
rep from * to 3 sts before m, yo, k2tog, k1, yo, sm, k1,
sm, yo, k1, k2tog, yo, **p2, yo, k3tog, yo; rep from **
to last 8 sts, p2, yo, k2tog, k1, yo, k3.

Row 8: Sl1, k3, *p1, k1, p1, k2; rep from * to 4 sts before
m, [p1, k1] twice, sm, p1, sm, [k1, p1] twice, **k2, p1,
k1, p1; rep from ** to last 4 sts, k4.

Row 9: Sl1, k2, yo, p1, *k1, p1, k1, p2; rep from * to 4 sts
before m, [k1, p1] twice, yo, sm, k1, sm, yo, [p1, k1]
twice, **p2, k1, p1, k1; rep from ** to last 4 sts, p1,
yo, k3.

Row 10: Sl1, k4, *p1, k1, p1, k2; rep from * to m, sm, p1,
sm, **k2, p1, k1, p1; rep from ** to last 5 sts, k5.

Row 11: Sl1, k2, yo, p2 *yo, k3tog, yo, p2; rep from * to
m, yo, sm, k1, sm, yo, **p2, yo, k3tog, yo; rep from **
to last 5 sts, p2, yo, k3.

Row 12: Sl1, k2, p1, k2, *p1, k1, p1, k2; rep from * to 1 st
before m, p1, sm, p1, sm, p1, **k2, p1, k1, p1; rep from
** to last 6 sts, k2, p1, k3.

Row 13: Sl1, k2, yo, k1, p2, *k1, p1, k1, p2; rep from * to
1 st before m, k1, yo, sm, k1, sm, yo, k1, **p2, k1, p1,
k1; rep from ** to last 6 sts, p2, k1, yo, k3.

Row 14: Sl1, k3, p1, k2, *p1, k1, p1, k2; rep from * to 2 sts
before m, p1, k1, sm, p1, sm, k1, p1, **k2, p1, k1, p1;
rep from ** to last 7 sts, k2, p1, k4.

Lace Chart

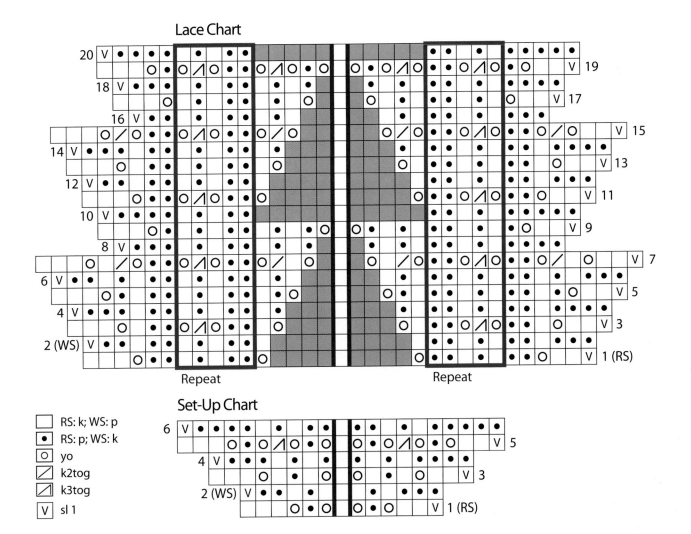

Repeat   Repeat

Set-Up Chart

	RS: k; WS: p
•	RS: p; WS: k
O	yo
╱	k2tog
⋀	k3tog
V	sl 1

Row 15: Sl1, k2, yo, k2tog, yo, p2, *yo, k3tog, yo, p2; rep from * to 2 sts before m, yo, k2tog, yo, sm, k1, sm, yo, k2tog, yo, **p2, yo, k3tog, yo; rep from ** to last 7 sts, p2, yo, k2tog, yo, k3.

Row 16: Sl1, k2, *p1, k1, p1, k2; rep from * to 3 sts before m, p1, k1, p1, sm, p1, sm, p1, k1, p1, **k2, p1, k1, p1; rep from ** to last 3 sts, k3.

Row 17: Sl1, k2, yo, *k1, p1, k1, p2; rep from * to 3 sts before m, k1, p1, k1, yo, sm, k1, sm, yo, k1, p1, k1, **p2, k1, p1, k1; rep from ** to last 3 st, yo, k3.

Row 18: Sl1, k3, *p1, k1, p1, k2; rep from * to 4 sts before m, [p1, k1] twice, sm, p1, sm, [k1, p1] twice, **k2, p1, k1, p1; rep from ** to last 4 sts, k4.

Row 19: Sl1, k2, yo, p1, *yo, k3tog, yo, p2; rep from * to 4 sts before m, yo, k3tog, yo, p1, yo, sm, k1, sm, yo, p1, yo, k3tog, yo, **p2, yo, k3tog, yo; rep from ** to last 4 sts, p1, yo, k3.

Row 20: Sl1, k4, *p1, k1, p1, k2; rep from * to m, sm, p1, sm, **k2, p1, k1, p1; rep from ** to last 5 sts, k5.

Finishing

Block to measurements.
Weave in ends.

Brandywine Tunic

Brandywine Tunic fulfills your wish for a graceful, elegant pullover with minimal shaping and textural stitches. Stunning cables accentuate the beauty of self-striping chunky yarn with an effortless sophistication, ensuring gorgeous style in the blink of an eye.

Sizes

Woman's XS (S, M, L, XL, 2XL, 3XL)

Finished Measurements

Bust circumference (seamed): 32 (36¼, 40½, 44¾, 49, 53¼, 57½)"/81.5 (92, 103, 113.5, 124.5, 135.5, 146) cm

Length: 25 (25, 25¾, 26¼, 27½, 27¾, 28¾)"/63.5 (63.5, 65.5, 68, 70, 70.5, 73) cm

Yarn

Plymouth Yarn Gina Chunky, bulky weight #5 yarn (100% wool; 131 yd/3.5 oz, 119 m/100 g per skein)
4 (4, 4, 5, 6, 6, 7) balls #0107 Gaelic

Needles and Other Materials

• US size 11 (8 mm) knitting needles or size needed to obtain gauge
• 24" (60 cm) circular knitting needle, US size 11 (8 mm) or size needed to obtain gauge
• US size 10 (6 mm) needles or size needed to obtain gauge
• 2 cable needles
• 4 stitch markers
• Tapestry needle

Finished Gauge

With US 11 (8 mm) needles, 15 sts x 17 rows in Climbing Cable patt, blocked = 4"/10 cm
With US 10 (6 mm) needles, 15 sts x 19 rows in St st, blocked = 4"/10 cm
Save time by taking time to check gauge.

Notes

• This pullover is worked flat and seamed after blocking, with the neckline added last and worked in the round.
• For parts worked in stockinette stitch, slip the first stitch of each row.
• Stitch patterns include selvedge stitches.

Special Stitches

2/2/2 LPC: Slip 2 sts to first cable needle and hold in front, slip 2 sts to second cable needle and hold in back, k2, p2 from second cable needle, k2 from first cable needle.

Stitch Patterns

Climbing Cable (multiple of 8 sts + 14)

Row 1 (WS): K1, p1, *k2, p2; rep from * to last 4 sts, k2, p1, k1.

Row 2 (RS): K2, *p2, k2; rep from * to end.

Rows 3–4: Rep Rows 1–2.

Row 5: K1, p1, *k2, p2; rep from * to last 4 sts, k2, p1, k1.

Row 6: K2, *p2, 2/2/2 LPC; rep from * to last 4 sts, p2, k2.

Rows 7–12: Rep Rows 1–2.

Row 13: K1, p1, *k2, p2; rep from * to last 4 sts, k2, p1, k1.

Row 14: [K2, p2] twice, *2/2/2 LPC, p2; rep from * to last 6 sts, k2, p2, k2.

Rows 15–16: Rep Rows 1–2.

Rep Rows 1–16 for patt.

Stockinette Stitch (St st)

Row 1 (RS): Sl1, knit to end.

Row 2 (WS): Sl1, purl to last st, k1.

Rep Rows 1–2 for patt.

Back

With larger straight needles, CO 62 (70, 78, 86, 94, 102, 110) sts.

Begin Climbing Cable patt and work even until back measures a finished length of 17 (17, 17½, 18, 18¼, 18¼, 18¾)"/43 (43, 44.5, 45.5, 46.5, 46.5, 47.5) cm from cast-on edge, ending with a WS row.

Change to smaller needles.

Next row (RS): Sl1, ssk, knit to last 3 sts, k2tog, k1—60 (68, 76, 84, 92, 100, 108) sts.

Next row (WS): Sl1, purl to last st, k1.

Place a removable (locking) stitch marker at the beginning and end of row to note beginning of armhole.

Continue in St st, slipping first st of every row and knitting last st of every row, until armhole measures a finished length of 6 (6, 6¼, 6¾, 7¼, 7½, 8)"/15 (15, 16, 17, 18.5, 19, 20.5) cm from stitch marker, ending with a WS row.

Climbing Cable

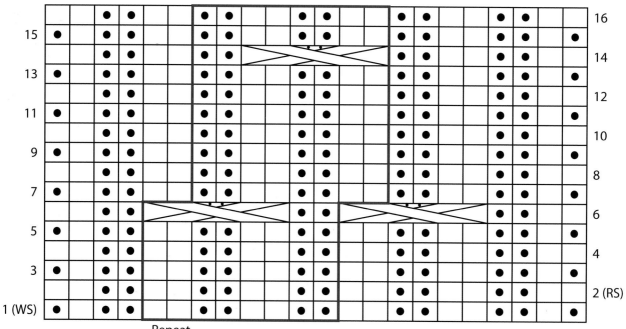

Repeat

☐ RS: k; WS: p

▣ RS: p; WS: k

▨ 2/2/2 LPC

Neck Shaping

Row 1 (RS): Work 20 (23, 26, 28, 30, 34, 38) sts, BO center 20 (22, 24, 28, 32, 32, 32) sts, then knit to end of the row.

Row 2 (WS): Work to neck edge, join new yarn on other side of shoulder, and work to end of row.

Working both sides of neck at same time, BO 4 (5, 6, 7, 7, 8, 8) sts at beg of each neck edge 1 (1, 2, 2, 1, 2, 2) time(s), then 5 (6, 0, 0, 8, 0, 0) sts at each neck edge once—11 (12, 14, 14, 15, 18, 22) sts rem on each side of neck.

Shoulder Shaping

BO 5 (6, 8, 8, 8, 9, 11) sts at beg of next 2 rows, then BO final 6 (6, 6, 6, 7, 9, 11) sts at beg of next 2 rows.

Front

With larger straight needles, CO 62 (70, 78, 86, 94, 102, 110) sts.

Begin Climbing Cable patt and work even until back measures a finished length of 17 (17, 17½, 18, 18¼, 18¼, 18¾)"/43 (43, 44.5, 45.5, 46.5, 46.5 47.5) cm from cast-on edge, ending with a WS row.

Change to smaller needles.

Next row (RS): K1, ssk, knit to last 3 sts, k2tog, k1—60 (68, 76, 84, 92, 100, 108) sts.

Next row (WS): K1, purl to last st, k1.

Place a removable (locking) stitch marker at the beginning and end of row to note beginning of armhole.

Continue in St st, slipping first st of every row and knitting last st of every row, until armhole measures a finished length of 4 (4, 4½, 5, 5½, 5¾, 6¼)"/10 (10, 11.5, 12.5, 14, 14.5,16) cm from stitch marker, ending with a WS row.

Finished Measurements

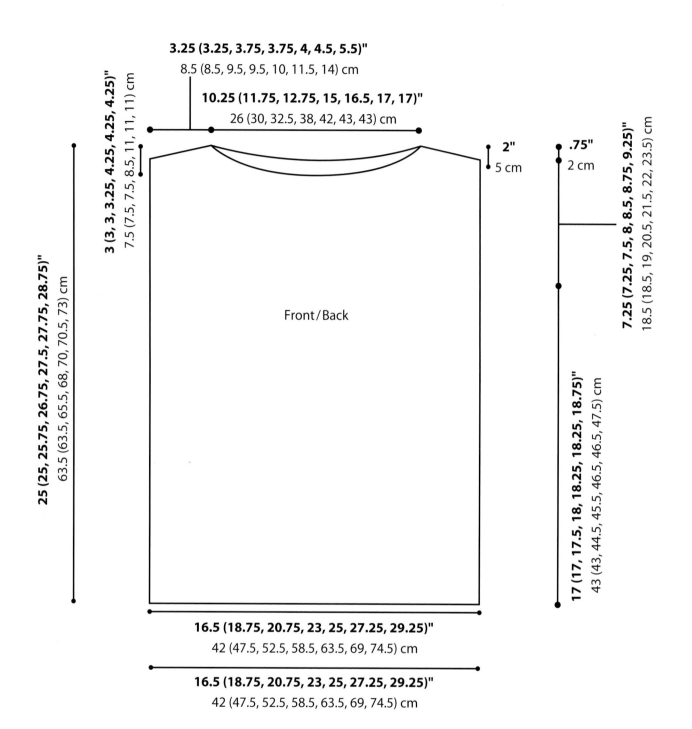

3.25 (3.25, 3.75, 3.75, 4, 4.5, 5.5)"
8.5 (8.5, 9.5, 9.5, 10, 11.5, 14) cm

10.25 (11.75, 12.75, 15, 16.5, 17, 17)"
26 (30, 32.5, 38, 42, 43, 43) cm

3 (3, 3, 3.25, 4.25, 4.25, 4.25)"
7.5 (7.5, 7.5, 8.5, 11, 11, 11) cm

25 (25, 25.75, 26.75, 27.5, 27.75, 28.75)"
63.5 (63.5, 65.5, 68, 70, 70.5, 73) cm

Front/Back

2"
5 cm

.75"
2 cm

7.25 (7.25, 7.5, 8, 8.5, 8.75, 9.25)"
18.5 (18.5, 19, 20.5, 21.5, 22, 23.5) cm

17 (17, 17.5, 18, 18.25, 18.25, 18.75)"
43 (43, 44.5, 45.5, 46.5, 46.5, 47.5) cm

16.5 (18.75, 20.75, 23, 25, 27.25, 29.25)"
42 (47.5, 52.5, 58.5, 63.5, 69, 74.5) cm

16.5 (18.75, 20.75, 23, 25, 27.25, 29.25)"
42 (47.5, 52.5, 58.5, 63.5, 69, 74.5) cm

Neck Shaping

Row 1 (RS): Work 20 (23, 26, 28, 30, 34, 38) sts, BO center
20 (22, 24, 28, 32, 32, 32) sts, then knit to end of row.

Row 2 (WS): Work to neck edge, join new yarn on other
side of shoulder, and work to end of row.

Working both sides of neck at same time, BO 2 (2, 3, 3,
3, 4, 4) sts at beg of each neck edge 3 (1, 4, 2, 1, 4, 4)
time(s), then 3 (3, 0, 4, 4, 0, 0) sts at each neck edge
1 (3, 0, 2, 3, 0, 0) times—11 (12, 14, 14, 15, 18, 22)
sts rem on each side of neck.

Work even for 4 rows, ending with a WS row.

Shoulder Shaping

BO 5 (6, 8, 8, 8, 9, 11) sts at beg of next 2 rows, then BO
final 6 (6, 6, 6, 7, 9, 11) sts at beg of next 2 rows.

Finishing

Weave in ends.

Block to measurements.

Sew shoulder seams. Sew side seams from hem to stitch
marker.

Neckband

With circular needles, pick up and knit 84 (96, 104, 120,
132, 136, 136) sts evenly around neck. Place marker
and join to work in the round.

Ribbing rnd: *K2, p2; rep from * to end of rnd.

Rep Ribbing rnd 4 times.

BO loosely in patt.

Weave in ends.

Isinglass Capelet

Skill Level: Easy

Diagonal knits and purls bordered by simple garter stitch draw the eye into the lush texture of this easy capelet. Large and plush, it can be pulled down over your shoulders for those chilly evenings or worn loose around the neck as a stylish accessory.

Finished Measurements
Width: 12"/30.5 cm before borders, 16"/40.5 cm with
    borders
Length: 40"/101.5 cm before seaming

Yarn
Premier Yarns Deborah Norville Serenity Chunky Heathers,
    bulky weight #5 yarn (100% acrylic; 109 yd/3.5 oz,
    99 m/100 g per skein)
    3 balls #750-01 Smoke Heather

Needles and Other Materials
• 32" (80 cm) circular knitting needle, US size 11 (8 mm)
    or size needed to obtain gauge
• Stitch marker
• Tapestry needle

Finished Gauge
10 sts x 19 rows in Texture Patt, blocked = 4"/10 cm
Save time by taking time to check gauge.

Notes
• This capelet is worked flat in one piece, then seamed
    closed.
• After seaming, the border is picked up around the
    edges and worked in the round.

Stitch Patterns
Texture Pattern (multiple of 4 sts + 2)
Row 1 (RS): K1, p1, *k2, p2; rep from * to last 4 sts, k2,
    p1, k1.
Row 2 (WS): K1, *k2, p2; rep from * to last st, k1.
Row 3: K2, *p2, k2; rep from * to end.
Row 4: K1, *p2, k2; rep from * to last st, k1.
Rep Rows 1–4 for patt.

Circular Garter
Rnd 1: Purl.
Rnd 2: Knit.
Rep Rnds 1–2 for patt.

Capelet

CO 30 sts.
Work Texture Patt until capelet measures a finished length
    of approx 40"/101.5 cm long, ending with a WS row.
BO on next RS row.

Finishing

Block to measurements.
Seam the ends together.

Borders
With RS facing, begin at seam and pick up 105 sts around
    top edge. Place marker and join to work in the round.
Work in Circular Garter patt until border measures 2"/5 cm
    from edge.
BO loosely.
Rep with bottom edge of capelet.
Block borders lightly, if desired.
Weave in ends.

East Twin Bracelet Set

Skill Level: **Easy**

Leftover yarn is put to good use with this set of charming, ultra-trendy bracelets. Playing with I-cord construction offers unique ways to layer up the wrists in color and fun.

Looped Bracelet is on the right.
Twisted Bracelet is on the left.

Finished Measurements

Adjustable to wrist circumference

Yarn

Plymouth Gina Chunky, bulky weight
#5 yarn (100% wool; 131 yd/3.5
oz, 120 m/100 g per skein)
Approx 25 yd/22 m #0107 Gaelic

Needles and Other Materials

• US size 9 (5.5 mm) set of 4 double-
pointed needles
• Tapestry needle

Special Stitch

I-cord: See page 96 for a photo
tutorial.

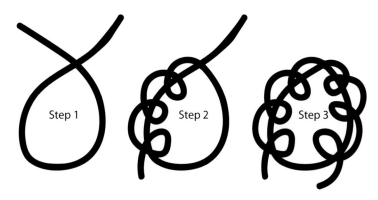

How to twist the Twisted Bracelet.

Looped Bracelet

CO 3 sts.
Work I-cord until it measures ¼"/.5 cm less than desired
circumference.
BO.
Rep for a second I-cord.
Fold first I-cord in half to form a loop. Fold second I-cord
in half over the first I-cord, forming a loop over it.
Knot the ends together.
Trim ends, as desired.

Twisted Bracelet

CO 3 sts.
Work I-cord until it measures 3 times larger than desired
wrist circumference.
BO.
Fold I-cord in half to form a small loop in the center,
approx ¼"/.5 cm larger than actual wrist circumference.
Twist overlapping ends around loop as shown in the
illustrations above and knot to secure ends.
Trim the ends, as desired.

Mazon Vest

Skill Level: **Intermediate**

This lightweight textured vest gives you plenty of layering possibilities while highlighting the cushy richness of the yarn. Easy to knit up and just as easy to wear, this modern vest is a must for year-round style.

Sizes

Woman's XS (S, M, L, XL, 2XL)

Finished Measurements

Bust (buttoned): 34³⁄₄ (37, 39¹⁄₂, 44, 46¹⁄₄, 46¹⁄₄)"/88.5 (94, 100.5, 112, 117.5, 117.5) cm

Length: 29 (29¹⁄₄, 29³⁄₄, 30¹⁄₂, 30¹⁄₂, 31¹⁄₄)"/73.5 (74.5, 75.5, 77.5, 77.5, 79.5) cm

Yarn

Patons Shetland Chunky Tweeds, bulky weight #5 yarn (72% acrylic, 25% wool, 3% viscose; 125 yd/3 oz, 114 m/85 g per skein)

5 (5, 6, 6, 7, 7) balls #7532 Deep Red Tweeds

Needles and Other Materials

- 24" (60 cm) circular knitting needle, US size 10 (6 mm) or size needed to obtain gauge
- 32" (80 cm) circular knitting needle, US size 10 (6 mm) or size needed to obtain gauge
- Stitch marker
- 1"/2.5 cm button
- Tapestry needle

Finished Gauge

14 sts x 21 rows in Diamond Patt, blocked = 4"/10 cm
Save time by taking time to check gauge.

Notes

- Body of vest is worked flat. Armhole trim is worked in the round.
- Stitch patterns include selvedge stitches.

Stitch Patterns

K2, P2 Rib (multiple of 4 sts + 2)

Row 1: K1, *k2, p2; rep from * to last st, k1.
Rep Row 1 for patt.

Diamond Pattern (multiple of 8 sts +2)

Row 1 and all odd-numbered rows (WS): K1, purl to last st, k1.
Row 2 (RS): K1, *p1, k7; rep from * to last st, k1.
Row 4: K1, *k1, p1, k5, p1; rep from * to last st, k1.
Row 6: K1, *k2, p1, k3, p1, k1; rep from * to last st, k1.
Row 8: K1, *k3, p1, k1, p1, k2; rep from * to last st, k1.
Row 10: K1, *k4, p1, k3; rep from * to last st, k1.
Row 12: Rep Row 8.
Row 14: Rep Row 6.
Row 16: Rep Row 4.
Rep Rows 1–16 for patt.

Back

CO 58 (66, 74, 74, 82, 82) sts.
Rows 1–16: Work K2, P2 Rib patt.
Change to Diamond Patt and work even until back measures a finished length of 20¹⁄₂"/51.5 cm from cast-on edge, ending with a WS row.

Shape Armhole

BO 3 (5, 6, 6, 6, 6) sts at beg of next 2 rows—52 (56, 62, 62, 70, 70) sts rem.

Dec row (RS): K1, ssk, work in patt to last 3 sts, k2tog, k1—2 sts dec'd.

Rep Dec row every RS row 1 (3, 4, 4, 5, 5) more time(s)—48 (48, 52, 52, 58, 58) sts rem.

Work even in est patt until armhole measures a finished length of 7½ (8, 8½, 9¼, 9¼, 10)"/19 (20.5, 21.5, 23.5, 23.5, 25.5) cm, ending with a WS row.

Shape Shoulders

BO 6 (6, 6, 6, 8, 8) sts at beg of next 2 rows, then 5 (5, 5, 6, 6) sts at beg of next 2 rows.

BO rem 26 (26, 30, 30, 30, 30) sts.

Left Front

CO 34 (34, 34, 42, 42, 42) sts.
Work as for Back to armhole.

Shape Armhole and Neck

Note: Neck and armhole are started and worked at the same time, so read this section carefully.

Row 1 (RS): BO 3 (5, 6, 6, 6, 6) sts at beg of armhole edge, work in patt to last 3 sts, k2tog [neck dec], k1—30 (28, 27, 35, 35, 35) sts.

Row 2 (WS): Work in est patt.

Dec row (RS): K1, ssk [armhole dec], work in patt to last 3 sts, k2tog [neck dec], k1—2 sts dec'd.

Continue to dec 1 st at beg of armhole every RS row 1 (3, 4, 4, 5, 5) more time(s), and *at the same time*, work

neck dec at end of every RS row 15 (6, 1, 15, 7, 5) times, then every *other* RS row 1 (6, 9, 3, 7, 9) times.

Work even on rem 11 (11, 11, 11, 14, 14) sts until armhole measures a finished length of 7½ (8, 8½, 9¼, 9¼, 10)"/19 (20.5, 21.5, 23.5, 23.5, 25.5) cm, ending with a WS row.

Shape Shoulders

BO 6 (6, 6, 6, 8, 8) sts at beg of next RS row, work even for 3 rows.

BO rem 5 (5, 5, 5, 6, 6) sts.

Right Front

CO 34 (34, 34, 42, 42, 42) sts.
Work as for Back to armhole.

Shape Armhole and Neck

Note: Neck and armhole are started and worked at the same time, so read this section carefully.

Row 1 (RS): K1, ssk [neck dec], work in patt to end—1 st dec'd at neck edge.

Row 2 (WS): BO 3 (5, 6, 6, 6, 6) sts at beg of armhole edge, work in patt to end—30 (28, 27, 35, 35, 35) sts.

Dec row (RS): K1, ssk [neck dec], work in patt to last 3 sts, k2tog [armhole dec], k1—2 sts dec'd.

Continue to dec 1 st at beg of neck edge every RS row 15 (6, 1, 15, 7, 5) times, then every *other* RS row 1 (6, 9, 3, 7, 9) times, and *at the same time*, work 1 armhole dec at end of every RS row 1 (3, 4, 4, 5, 5) more time(s).

Work even on rem 11 (11, 11, 11, 14, 14) sts until armhole measures a finished length of 7½ (8, 8½, 9¼, 9¼, 10)"/19 (20.5, 21.5, 23.5, 23.5, 25.5) cm, ending with a RS row.

Finished Measurements

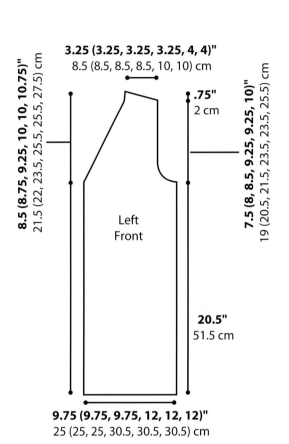

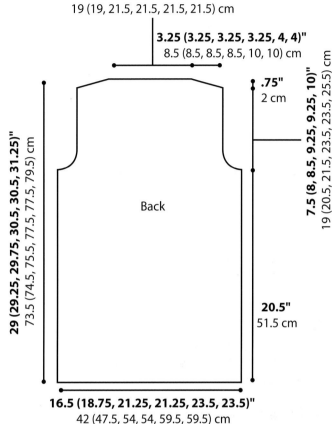

Shape Shoulders

BO 6 (6, 6, 6, 8, 8) sts at beg of next WS row, work even
for 3 rows.
BO rem 5 (5, 5, 5, 6, 6) sts.

Finishing

Weave in ends.
Block to schematic measurements.
Sew shoulder seams together. Sew side seams.

Armhole Trim

With 24" (60 cm) circular needle, beg at underarm with RS
facing and pick up and knit 65 (72, 79, 85, 83, 89) sts
evenly around armhole.
Purl 1 row.
BO knitwise.

Front and Neck Trim

With 32"/80 cm circular needle, beg at lower right front
edge, pick up and knit 80 sts along edge to neckline,
place marker, pick up and knit 30 (32, 33, 36, 36, 39)
sts along right front neck to shoulder, pick up and knit
26 (26, 30, 30, 30, 30) sts along back neck, pick up and
knit 30 (32, 33, 36, 36, 39) sts along left front neck,
pick up and knit 80 sts to left lower front edge—246
(250, 256, 262, 262, 268) sts.

Next row (WS): Knit to marker, use the cable-cast on to
CO 6 sts for button loop, knit to end.

BO knitwise on next row.

Sew on button to coordinate with button loop.

Weave in ends.

Lynnhaven Cowl

Skill Level: **Easy**

Rich texture and super soft yarn come together in a cowl that is squishy, warm, and beautiful to wear. If you like, you can pair it with the matching Lynnhaven Headband (see page 53).

Finished Measurements
Circumference (after seaming): 26"/66 cm
Width: 9¾"/25 cm

Yarn
Knit Picks Biggo, super bulky weight #6 yarn (50% super-
wash merino, 50% nylon; 110 yd/3.5 oz, 100 m/100 g
per skein)
2 skeins #25616 Duchess Heather

Needles and Other Materials
• US size 11 (8 mm) knitting needles or size needed to
obtain gauge
• Tapestry needle

Finished Gauge
12 sts x 19 rows in Seed Column Patt, blocked = 4"/10 cm
Save time by taking time to check gauge.

Note
• The cowl is worked flat before seaming.

Stitch Pattern
Seed Column Pattern (multiple of 9 sts + 7)
Row 1 (RS): Sl1, *[p1, k1] twice, p1, k1 tbl, p2, k1 tbl; rep
from * to last 6 sts, [p1, k1] 3 times.
Row 2 (WS): Sl1, *[p1, k1] twice, p1, p1 tbl, k2, p1 tbl; rep
from * to last 6 sts, [p1, k1] twice, p2.
Rep Rows 1–2 for patt.

Cowl

CO 34 sts.
Work Seed Column Patt until piece measures approx 26"/66 cm from cast-on edge, ending with a RS row.
BO.

Finishing

Block to schematic measurements.
Sew cast-on edge to the bind-off edge.
Weave in ends.

Lynnhaven Headband

Skill Level: **Easy**

Pair this simple headband up with the Lynnhaven Cowl (also shown in the photo) or wear it on its own. Either way, with its seed stitch pattern and long ties, this charming accessory is just the ticket for taming flyaway hair.

Finished Measurements

Length (not including ties): 10"/25.5 cm
Width: 3"/7.5 cm

Yarn

Knit Picks Biggo, super bulky weight #6 yarn (50% super-
wash merino, 50% nylon; 110 yd/3.5 oz, 100 m/100 g
per skein)
1 skein of #25616 Duchess Heather

Needles and Other Materials

• US size 11 (8 mm) knitting needles or size needed to
obtain gauge
• Tapestry needle

Finished Gauge

12 sts x 19 rows in Seed Column Patt, blocked = 4"/10 cm
Save time by taking time to check gauge.

Special Stitches

s2kp: Slip next 2 sts together knitwise, k1, pass slipped sts
over—2 sts dec. For a photo tutorial, see page 94.

Stitch Pattern

Seed Column Pattern

Row 1 (RS): Sl1, k1, k1 tbl, [p1, k1] twice, p1, k1 tbl,
k1, p1.
Row 2 (WS): Sl1, p1, p1 tbl, [p1, k1] twice, p1, p1 tbl,
p1, k1.
Rep Rows 1–2 for patt.

Band

CO 3 sts.

Set-up row (WS): Sl1, p2.

Row 1 (RS): Sl1, M1, p1, M1, k1—5 sts.

Row 2 (WS): Sl1, [k1, p1] twice.

Row 3: Sl1, M1, k1, p1, k1, M1, k1—7 sts.

Row 4: Sl1, [p1, k1] twice, p2.

Row 5: Sl1, M1, [p1, k1] twice, p1, M1, k1—9 sts.

Row 6: Sl1, p1 tbl, [p1, k1] twice, p1, p1 tbl, p1.

Row 7: Sl1, M1, k1 tbl, [p1, k1] twice, p1, k1 tbl, M1, k1—11 sts.

Row 8: Sl1, p1, p1 tbl, [p1, k1] twice, p1, p1 tbl, p1, k1.

Beginning with Row 1, continue in Seed Column Patt until headband measures a finished length of approx 8¼"/21 cm from cast-on edge, ending with a WS row.

Row 1 (RS): Sl1, ssk, [p1, k1] twice, p1, k2tog, k1—9 sts.

Row 2 (WS): Sl1, p1, [p1, k1] twice, p3.

Row 3: Sl1, ssk, k1, p1, k1, k2tog, k1—7 sts.

Row 4: Sl1, [p1, k1] twice, p2.

Row 5: Sl1, ssk, p1, k2tog, k1—5 sts.

Row 6: Sl1, p4.

Row 7: Sl1, s2kp, k1—3 sts.

BO on next WS row.

Finishing

Weave in ends.
Block lightly.

Ties

Cut 4 lengths of yarn about 30"/76 cm long. Thread 2 strands of yarn through a tapestry needle. Insert needle into cast-on edge of headband. Remove needle from the strands and adjust the length so that the ends align. Holding two strands together and leaving the other two strands as singles, braid the strand to approx 4"/10 cm from end. Tie in a knot to secure. Repeat with bind-off edge of headband. Trim ends as needed. Weave in ends.

Cahaba Hat

Skill Level: Easy

Knit and purl stitches
swirl around the crown
of this hat, resulting
in a luscious, easy
texture that delights.
The chunky weight
promises a quick knit,
while the easy pattern
warms any time of the
year. Pair it up with
Cahaba Mitts (see page
59) for the perfect fall
ensemble!

Sizes

Adult S (L)

Finished Measurements

Circumference: 18¾ (21¾)"/47.5 (55) cm

Length to crown: 8¼ (9)"/21 (23) cm

Yarn

Bernat Softee Chunky, bulky weight #5 yarn (100% acrylic;
108 yd/3.5 oz, 99 m/100 g per skein)
1 ball #8114 Faded Denim

Needles and Other Materials

• 16" (40 cm) circular knitting needle, US size 11 (8 mm) or
size needed to obtain gauge
• US size 11 (8 mm) set of 4 double-pointed needles or size
needed to obtain gauge
• Stitch marker
• Tapestry needle

Finished Gauge

11 sts x 14 rows in Texture Purl Patt, blocked = 4"/10 cm

Save time by taking time to check gauge.

Note

• The hat is worked from the brim to the crown. Start with
the circular needle and switch to dpns when necessary.

Stitch Patterns

K2, P2 Rib (multiple of 4 sts)

Rnd 1: *K2, p2; rep from * to end of rnd.

Rep Rnd 1 for patt.

Texture Purl Pattern (multiple of 4 sts)

Rnd 1: *P1, k3; rep from * to end of rnd.

Rnd 2: *K1, p1, k2; rep from * to end of rnd.

Rnd 3: *K2, p1, k1; rep from * to end of rnd.

Rnd 4: *K3, p1; rep from * to end of rnd.

Rep Rnds 1–4 for patt.

Hat

Using circular needle, CO 52 (60) sts. Place marker and join
for working in the round.

Rnds 1–4: Work K2, P2 Rib patt.

Change to Texture Purl Patt and work even until hat measures a finished length of approx 6¼ (7)"/ 16 (18) cm
from cast-on edge.

Crown Shaping

Rnd 1: *Work in patt for 2 sts, k2tog; rep from * to end of rnd—39 (45) sts rem.

Rnds 2 and 4: Work in established patt.

Rnd 3: *Work in patt for 1 st, k2tog; rep from * to end of rnd—26 (30) sts rem.

Rnd 5: [K2tog] to end of rnd—13 (15) sts rem.

Rnd 6: Knit.

Rnd 7: [K2tog] 6 (7) times, k1—7 (8) sts rem.

Rnd 8: Knit.

Cut 8"/20.5 cm tail, draw through remaining stitches, and pull tight.

Weave in ends.

Cahaba Mitts

Skill Level: Easy

These effortless fingerless mitts, with beginner shaping and snug fit, exude rich, comforting texture. You'll love the satisfying instant gratification that comes from whipping these out in a couple of hours. Pair them up with the Cahaba Hat (see page 56) for the perfect fall ensemble!

Sizes
Adult S (L)

Finished Measurements
Circumference: 5¾ (7¼)"/14.5 (18.5) cm
Length: 12¼"/31 cm

Yarn
Bernat Softee Chunky, bulky weight #5 yarn (100% acrylic;
    108 yd/3.5 oz, 99 m/100 g per skein)
    1 ball #8114 Faded Denim

Needles and Other Materials
- US size 11 (8 mm) set of 4 double-pointed needles or size
  needed to obtain gauge
- Stitch marker
- Tapestry needle

Finished Gauge
11 sts x 14 rows in Texture Purl Patt, blocked = 4"/10 cm
Save time by taking time to check gauge.

Special Stitches
kfbf: Knit into the front, the back, and the front of the st—
    2 sts inc. See page 92 for a photo tutorial.
kfb: Knit into the front and back of the st—1 st inc. See
    page 91 for a photo tutorial.

Stitch Patterns
K2, P2 Rib (multiple of 4 sts)
Rnd 1: *K2, p2; rep from * to end of rnd.
Rep Rnd 1 for patt.

Texture Purl Pattern (multiple of 4 sts)
Rnd 1: *P1, k3; rep from * to end of rnd.
Rnd 2: *K1, p1, k2; rep from * to end of rnd.
Rnd 3: *K2, p1, k1; rep from * to end of rnd.
Rnd 4: *K3, p1; rep from * to end of rnd.
Rep Rnds 1–4 for patt.

Cuff

CO 16 (20) sts, dividing them evenly between the dpns. Place marker and join for working in the round, taking care not to twist sts.

Rnds 1–4: Work K2, P2 Rib.

Change to Texture Purl Patt and work even until cuff measures a finished length of approx 6½"/16.5 cm from cast-on edge.

Thumb Gusset

Rnd 1: Kfbf, work in patt to end of rnd—18 (22) sts.

Rnd 2: K2, place marker (m), work in patt to end of rnd.

Rnd 3: Knit to m, work in patt to end of rnd.

Rnd 4: Kfb, kfb, work in patt to end of rnd—4 sts before m.

Rnds 5–6: Knit to m, work in patt to end of rnd.

Rnd 7: Kfb, work to 1 st before m, kfb, work in patt to end of rnd—6 sts before m.

Rnds 8–9: Knit to m, work in patt to end of rnd.

Rnd 10: BO first 6 sts, work in patt to end of rnd—16 (20) sts rem.

Rnd 11: Rejoin mitt to beginning of rnd over gap of bind-off sts and work to end of rnd in patt.

Rnds 12–13: Work even in patt.

Rnds 14–17: Work K2, P2 Rib.

BO very loosely.

Finishing

Weave in ends.

Saluda Hood

Skill Level: **Easy**

Plush, simple, and charming, this hooded cowl keeps you warm on chilly days. Garter stitch ensures the utmost ease, while enhancing the luxurious squish of the chunky weight yarn.

Finished Measurements

Circumference (buttoned): 20"/51 cm
Hood length from cowl: 16"/40.5 cm
Cowl length: 8¼"/21 cm

Yarn

Lion Brand Woolspun, bulky weight #5 yarn (80% acrylic,
    20% wool; 127 yd/3.5 oz, 116 m/100 g per skein)
    3 balls #671-133 Rust

Needles and Other Materials

• 24" (60 cm) circular knitting needle, US size 11 (8 mm)
    or size needed to obtain gauge
• Four 1"/2.5 cm buttons
• Tapestry needle

Finished Gauge

11 sts x 22 rows in garter st, blocked = 4"/10 cm
Save time by taking time to check gauge.

Notes

• The cowl is worked flat. A circular needle is used to
    accommodate the number of stitches; do not join.
• See page 97 for a photo tutorial on 3-needle bind-off.

Cowl

CO 55 sts.
Rows 1–5: Knit.
Buttonhole row (RS): K3, yo, k2tog, knit to end.
Continue to knit every row and rep Buttonhole row every
    tenth row 3 times.
Knit 4 rows, ending with a WS row.

Shape Hood

Row 1 (RS): BO 2 sts, knit to end—53 sts.
Row 2 (WS): BO 2 sts, knit to end—51 sts.
Dec row (RS): K1, ssk, knit to last 3 sts, k2tog, k1—49 sts.
Knit 1 row.
Rep Dec row—47 sts.
Continue working in garter st until hood measures
    15¾"/40 cm from first BO row, ending with a WS row.
Next row: Knit to last 3 sts, k2tog, k1—46 sts.
Divide stitches evenly between two needles and close top
    of hood with 3-needle bind-off.

Finishing

Block as desired.
Sew buttons to correspond with buttonholes.
Weave in ends.

Genessee Vest

Skill Level: Intermediate

Genessee Vest is beautifully versatile and perfect for layering on those cooler days. The lace is sweetly simple while the construction is a breeze!

Sizes
Woman's XS (S, M, L, XL, 2XL, 3XL)

Finished Measurements
Bust: 30 (34, 38, 42, 46, 50, 54)"/76 (86.5, 96.5, 106.5,
117, 127, 137) cm
Back length: 20¼ (20¼, 21, 21, 21¾, 21¾, 21¾)"/51.5
(51.5, 53.5, 53.5, 55, 55, 55) cm

Yarn
Lion's Pride Woolspun, bulky weight #5 yarn (80% acrylic,
20% wool; 127 yd/3.5 oz, 116 m/100 g per skein)
4 (4, 5, 5, 5, 5, 5) skeins #671-099 Linen

Needles and Other Materials
• US size 11 (8 mm) knitting needles or size needed to
obtain gauge
• 16" (40 cm) circular knitting needle, US size 11 (8 mm)
or size needed to obtain gauge
• Stitch marker
• Tapestry needle

Finished Gauge
11 sts x 14 rows in St st, blocked = 4"/10 cm
10 sts x 15 rows in Simple Lace patt, blocked = 4"/10 cm
Save time by taking time to check gauge.

Notes
• This vest is worked in one long piece, from side to side.
• Stitch patterns include selvedge stitches.
• See page 90 for a photo tutorial on cable cast-on.

Stitch Patterns
Simple Lace (multiple of 4 sts)
Row 1 (RS): K2, *yo, k2tog, k2; rep from * to last 2 sts, k2.
Rows 2 and 4 (WS): K2, purl to last 2 sts, k2.
Row 3: K2, *k2, yo, k2tog; rep from * to last 2 sts, k2.
Rep Rows 1–4 for patt.

Bordered Stockinette Stitch (multiple of 1 st + 4)
Row 1 (WS): K2, purl to last 2 sts, k2.
Row 2 (RS): Knit.
Rep Rows 1–2 for patt.

Right Front

With straight needles, CO 56 (56, 56, 60, 60, 60, 60) sts.
Set-up row (WS): K2, purl to last 2 sts, k2.
Begin Simple Lace patt and work even until right front
measures a finished length of 13"/33 cm from cast-on
edge, ending with a WS row.

Change to Bordered St st patt and work even until right front measures a finished length of 17 (17½, 18¼, 18¾, 18¾, 19¼, 19¼)"/43 (44.5, 46.5, 47.5, 47.5, 49, 49) cm from cast-on edge, ending with a WS row.

Shape Right Armhole

Row 1 (RS): K10, loosely BO 20 (20, 20, 24, 24, 24, 26) sts, knit to end—36 (36, 36, 36, 36, 36, 34) sts.

Row 2 (WS): K2, purl 24 (24, 24, 24, 24, 24, 22) sts, cable cast-on 20 (20, 20, 24, 24, 24, 26) sts, purl to last 2 sts, k2—56 (56, 56, 60, 60, 60, 60) sts.

Place a stitch marker at beg of last row worked to indicate side.

Back

Continue in Bordered St st until back measures a finished length of 17¼ (17¼, 17¾, 18¼, 18¼, 18¾, 19½)"/44 (44, 45, 46.5, 46.5, 47.5, 49.5) cm from stitch marker, ending with a WS row.

Shape Left Armhole

Row 1 (RS): K10, loosely BO 20 (20, 20, 24, 24, 24, 26) sts, knit to end—36 (36, 36, 36, 36, 36, 34) sts.

Row 2 (WS): K2, purl 24 (24, 24, 24, 24, 24, 22) sts, cable cast-on 20 (20, 20, 24, 24, 24, 26) sts, purl to last 2 sts, k2—56 (56, 56, 60, 60, 60, 60) sts.

Remove first stitch marker and place at end of last row worked.

Left Front

Continue in Bordered St st until left front measures 4 (4½, 5¼, 5¾, 5¾, 6¼, 6¼)"/10 (11.5, 13.5, 14.5, 14.5, 16, 16) cm from stitch marker, ending with a WS row.

Change to Simple Lace patt and work even until piece measures 17 (17½, 18¼, 18¾, 18¾, 19¼, 19¼)"/43 (44.5, 46.5, 47.5, 47.5, 49, 49) cm from stitch marker, ending with a WS row.

BO loosely.

Finished Measurements

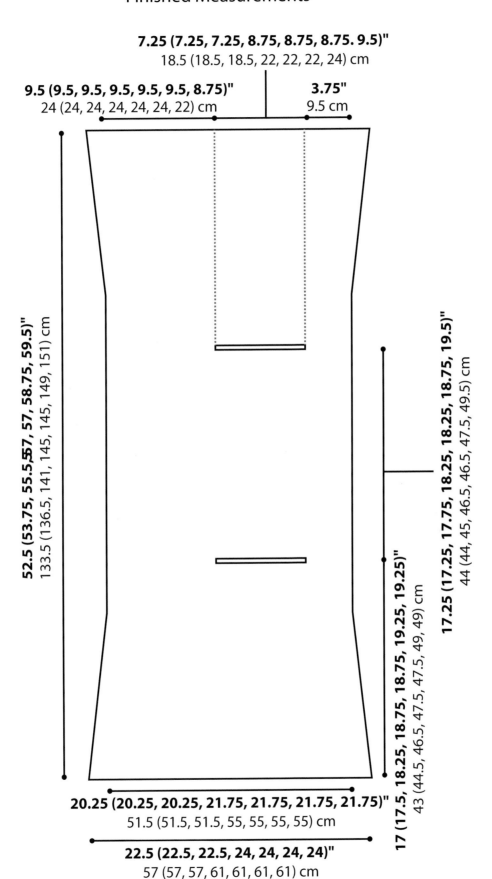

7.25 (7.25, 7.25, 8.75, 8.75, 8.75. 9.5)"
18.5 (18.5, 18.5, 22, 22, 22, 24) cm

9.5 (9.5, 9.5, 9.5, 9.5, 9.5, 8.75)"
24 (24, 24, 24, 24, 24, 22) cm

3.75"
9.5 cm

52.5 (53.75, 55.5,57, 57, 58.75, 59.5)"
133.5 (136.5, 141, 145, 145, 149, 151) cm

17.25 (17.25, 17.75, 18.25, 18.25, 18.75, 19.5)"
44 (44, 45, 46.5, 46.5, 47.5, 49.5) cm

17 (17.5, 18.25, 18.75, 18.75, 19.25, 19.25)"
43 (44.5, 46.5, 47.5, 47.5, 49, 49) cm

20.25 (20.25, 20.25, 21.75, 21.75, 21.75, 21.75)"
51.5 (51.5, 51.5, 55, 55, 55, 55) cm

22.5 (22.5, 22.5, 24, 24, 24, 24)"
57 (57, 57, 61, 61, 61, 61) cm

Note the edging around the armhole, made by picking up the stitches and purling one round.

Armhole Edging

With circular needle, pick up 42 (42, 46, 50, 50, 50, 54) sts evenly around armhole. Place marker and join for working in the round.
Purl 1 rnd.
BO knitwise.
Rep for other armhole.

Finishing

Weave in all ends.
Block to measurements.

Baker Slouch Hat

Skill Level: **Intermediate**

Highlight your self-striping yarn with subtle, soft cables and delicate ribbing for a look that is romantic and snug. Baker Slouch Hat is lovely in both its texture and elegance without sacrificing any of its warmth or simplicity.

Sizes
One size fits most

Finished Measurements
Circumference at opening: 19¾"/50 cm
Length to crown: 12"/30.5 cm

Yarn
Universal Yarns Poems Chunky, bulky weight #5 yarn
  (100% wool; 110 yd/3.5 oz, 100 m/100 g per skein)
  2 balls #901 Embers

Needles and Other Materials
• 16" (40 cm) circular knitting needle, US size 10 (6 mm)
  or size needed to obtain gauge
• US size 10 (6 mm) set of 4 double-pointed needles or
  size needed to obtain gauge
• Cable needle
• Stitch marker
• Tapestry needle

Finished Gauge
20 sts x 24 rows in Double Cable Patt, blocked = 4"/10 cm
Save time by taking time to check gauge.

Note
• Hat is worked in the round from the brim to the crown.
  Start with circular needle, then switch to dpns when
  necessary.

Special Stitches
2/1 LPC: Slip 2 sts to cable needle and hold in front, p1,
  k2 from cable needle.
2/1 RPC: Slip 1 st to cable needle and hold in back, k2, p1
  from cable needle.
2/2 LC: Slip 2 sts to cable needle and hold in front, k2, k2
  from cable needle.

Double Cable Pattern

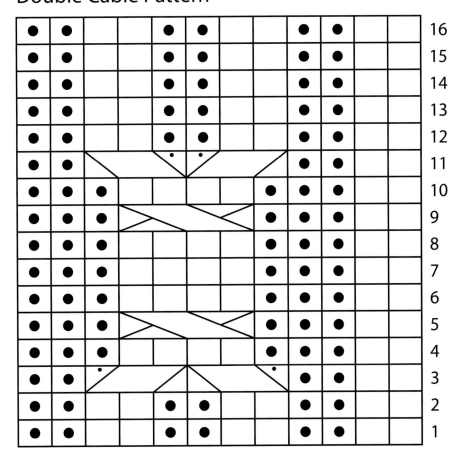

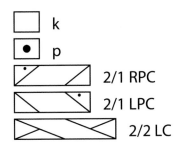

	k
	p
	2/1 RPC
	2/1 LPC
	2/2 LC

Stitch Pattern

Double Cable Pattern (multiple of 12 sts)

Rnds 1–2: *K2, p2; rep from * to end of rnd.

Rnd 3: *K2, p2, 2/1 LPC, 2/1 RPC, p2; rep from * to end of rnd.

Rnd 4: *K2, p3, k4, p3; rep from * to end of rnd.

Rnd 5: *K2, p3, 2/2 LC, p3; rep from * to end of rnd.

Rnds 6–8: *K2, p3, k4, p3; rep from * to end of rnd.

Rnd 9: *K2, p3, 2/2 LC, p3; rep from * to end of rnd.

Rnd 10: *K2, p3, k4, p3; rep from * to end of rnd.

Rnd 11: *K2, p2, 2/1 RPC, 2/1 LPC, p2; rep from * to end of rnd.

Rnds 12–16: *K2, p2; rep from * to end of rnd.

Rep Rnds 1–16 for patt.

Hat

Using circular needle, CO 99 sts. Place marker and join for working in the round.

Rnd 1: *K1, p2, k2, p2, k2, p2; rep from * to end of rnd.

Rnds 2–9: Rep Rnd 1.

Rnd 10 (inc rnd): *K1, M1, p2, k2, p2, k2, p2; rep from * to end of rnd—108 sts.

Change to Double Cable Patt and work even until hat measures a finished length of approx 10"/40.5 cm from cast-on edge.

Crown Shaping

Note: In the following rnds, if working in patt does not leave you enough sts to complete a called-for cable, purl each purl and knit each knit.

Rnd 1: *Work in patt for 10 sts, k2tog; rep from * to end of rnd—99 sts.

Rnd 2: *Work in patt for 9 sts, k2tog; rep from * to end of rnd—90 sts.

Rnd 3: *Work in patt for 8 sts, k2tog; rep from * to end of rnd—81 sts.

Rnd 4: *Work in patt for 7 sts, k2tog; rep from * to end of rnd—72 sts.

Rnd 5: *Work in patt for 6 sts, k2tog; rep from * to end of rnd—63 sts.

Rnd 6: *Work in patt for 5 sts, k2tog; rep from * to end of rnd—54 sts.

Rnd 7: *Work in patt for 4 sts, k2tog; rep from * to end of rnd—45 sts.

Rnd 8: *Work in patt for 3 sts, k2tog; rep from * to end of rnd—36 sts.

Rnd 9: *Work in patt for 2 sts, k2tog; rep from * to end of rnd—27 sts.

Rnd 10: *Work in patt for 1 st, k2tog; rep from * to end of rnd—18 sts.

Rnd 11: K2tog around—9 sts.

Rnd 12: Knit.

Cut 8"/20.5 cm tail, draw through remaining stitches, and pull tight.

Finishing

Weave in ends.
Block to measurements, as desired.

Mojave Cowl

Skill Level: **Intermediate**

Wrapped stitches add a unique effect, ramping up the texture and increasing the knitting fun. Combined with self-striping yarn, the results are charmingly rustic, yet oh so trendy.

Finished Measurements
Length (after seaming): 47½"/120.5 cm
Width: 6"/15 cm

Yarn
Lion Brand Tweed Stripes, bulky weight #5 yarn (100% acrylic; 144 yd/3 oz, 132 m/100 g per skein)
2 balls #753-216 Ozark Forest

Needles and Other Materials
• US size 10 (6 mm) knitting needles or size needed to obtain gauge
• Tapestry needle

Finished Gauge
22 sts x 25 rows in Wrap Patt, blocked = 4"/10 cm
Save time by taking time to check gauge.

Special Stitch
Wrap3: Lift third stitch on left needle up and over first 2 sts and off needle, k1, yo, k1.

Stitch Pattern
Wrap Pattern (multiple of 5 sts + 4)
Row 1 (RS): Sl1, p2, *k3, p2; rep from * to last st, k1.
Row 2 (WS): Sl1, *p2, k3; rep from * to last 3 sts, p2, k1.
Row 3: Sl1, p2, *Wrap3, p2; rep from * to last st, k1.
Row 4: Rep Row 2.
Row 5: Sl1, p2, *k3, p2; rep from * to last st, k1.
Row 6: Rep Row 2.
Rep Rows 1–6 for patt.

Cowl

CO 34 sts.
Work Wrap Patt until cowl measures approx 47½"/120.5 cm or to desired length, ending with Row 6.
BO loosely.

Finishing

Block to length.
Seam ends together. Weave in ends.

Kenai Cowl

Skill Level: **Easy**

Short and sweet, this
easy cowl featuring
gentle purl-ridge
chevrons is a snap
to whip up. Hugging
close to the neck, it
ensures deliciously
soft warmth and
relaxed comfort.

Finished Measurements
Length (before buttons): 20"/51 cm
Width: 8¾"/22 cm

Yarn
Lion Brand Homespun USA, super
   bulky weight #6 yarn (100%
   acrylic; 81 yd/5 oz, 74 m/100 g
   per skein)
   1 ball #135-148 Portland Wine

Needles and Other Materials
• US size 13 (9 mm) knitting needles
   or size needed to obtain gauge
• Five 1⅛"/3 cm buttons
• Tapestry needle

Finished Gauge
11 sts x 14 rows in Chevron Patt,
   blocked = 4"/10 cm
*Save time by taking time to check
   gauge.*

Stitch Pattern
Chevron Pattern
(multiple of 10 sts + 4)
Row 1 (RS): K2, [p1, k9] twice, k2.
Row 2 (WS): K2, [k1, p7, k1, p1]
   twice, k2.
Row 3: K2, [k2, p1, k5, p1, k1]
   twice, k2.
Row 4: K2, [p2, k1, p3, k1, p3]
   twice, k2.
Row 5: K2, [k4, p1, k1, p1, k3]
   twice, k2.
Row 6: K2, [p4, k1, p5] twice, k2.
Rep Rows 1–6 for patt.

Chevron Pattern

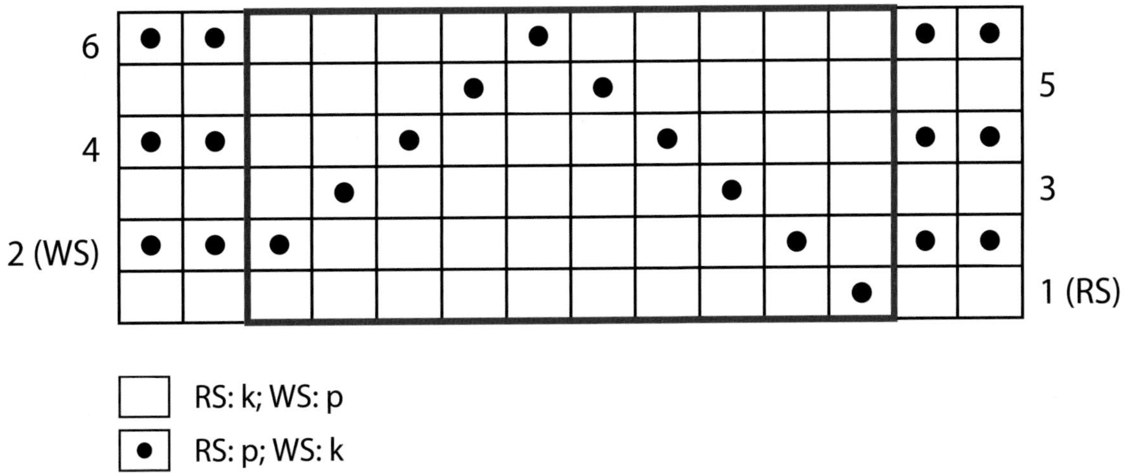

RS: k; WS: p

● RS: p; WS: k

Cowl

CO 24 sts.

Knit 2 rows.

Buttonhole row (WS): K4, [yo, k2tog, k2] 5 times.

Knit 2 rows.

Change to Chevron Patt and work even for 10 repeats
   total, ending with Row 6.

Knit 4 rows.

BO.

Finishing

Block to measurements.

Sew on buttons. Weave in ends.

Byram Shawl

Skill Level: Intermediate

The interplay of colors is beautifully accentuated with the openwork and subtle garter stitch texture, resulting in a wrap that is as lightweight as it looks. The asymmetrical shape is perfect for covering the shoulders or wearing like a scarf.

Finished Measurements

Wingspan: 65"/165 cm
Depth: 24"/61 cm

Yarn

Universal Cirrus Cotton, bulky weight #5 yarn (82%
    cotton, 18% polyamide; 109 yd/1.75 oz, 99 m/100 g
    per skein)
3 balls #206 Autumnal

Needles and Other Materials

• 24" (60 cm) circular knitting needle, US size 11 (8 mm)
    or size needed to obtain gauge
• Tapestry needle

Finished Gauge

8 sts x 14 rows in Garter Lace st, blocked = 4"/10 cm
Save time by taking time to check gauge.

Note

• This shawl is worked sideways in an asymmetrical shape,
    from side to side.

Stitch Pattern

Garter Lace (multiple of 2 sts + 2)
Row 1 (RS): Sl1, purl to last st, k1.
Row 2 (WS): Sl1, purl to last st, k1.
Row 3: Sl1, *yo, ssk; rep from * to last st, k1.
Row 4: Sl1, purl to last st, k1.
Rep Rows 1–4 for patt.

Shawl Body

CO 3 sts.
Row 1 (RS): K3.
Row 2 (WS): Sl1, kfb, k1—4 sts.
Row 3: Sl1, p2, k1.
Row 4: Sl1, p1, pfb, k1—5 sts.
Row 5: Sl1, k1, yo, ssk, k1.
Row 6: Sl1, purl to last 2 sts, pfb, k1—6 sts.
Row 7: Sl1, purl to last st, k1.
Row 8: Sl1, purl to last 2 sts, pfb, k1—7 sts.
Row 9: Sl1, k1, *yo, ssk; rep from * to last st, k1.
Row 10: Sl1, purl to last 2 sts, pfb, k1—8 sts.
Rep [Rows 7–10] 38 more times until there are 84 sts,
    ending with Row 10.

Border

Change to k2, p2 rib as follows:

Row 1 (RS): Sl1, *k2, p2; rep from * to last 3 sts, k3.

Row 2 (WS): Sl1, *p2, k2; rep from * to last 3 sts, p1, pfb, k1—85 sts.

Row 3: Sl1, p1, *k2, p2; rep from * to last 3 sts, k3.

Row 4: Sl1, *p2, k2; rep from * to last 4 sts, p2, kfb, k1—86 sts.

Row 5: Sl1, p2, *k2, p2; rep from * to last 3 sts, k3.

Row 6: Sl1, *p2, k2; rep from * to last 5 sts, p2, k1, kfb, k1—87 sts.

Row 7: Sl1, k1, p2, *k2, p2; rep from * to last 3 sts, k3.

Row 8: Sl1, *p2, k2; rep from * to last 2 sts, pfb, k1—88 sts.

Rep Rows 1–8.

Rep Rows 1–4—94 sts.

BO loosely.

Finishing

Block to measurements. Weave in ends.

Blue Harbor Scarf

Skill Level: **Intermediate**

Thick, chunky cables wind their way up through this scarf, letting you explore a rich world of criss-crossing stitches. The results are sumptuous and chic—an accessory that looks great with any wardrobe!

Finished Measurements
Length: 60"/152.5 cm
Width: 5¼"/13 cm

Yarn
Universal Yarn Uptown Bulky, bulky weight #5 yarn
    (100% acrylic; 87 yd/3.5 oz, 80 m/100 g per skein)
    2 balls #412 Sapphire

Needles and Other Materials
• US size 13 (9 mm) knitting needles or size needed
  to obtain gauge
• 2 cable needles
• Tapestry needle

Finished Gauge
14 sts x 16 rows in Cable Columns Patt, blocked
    = 4"/10 cm
Save time by taking time to check gauge.

Special Stitches
1/1 RC: Slip 1 st to cable needle and hold in back, k1, k1
    from cable needle.
2/1/2 RPC: Slip 2 sts to first cable needle and hold in back,
    slip 1 st to second cable needle and hold in back, k2, p1
    from second cable needle, k2 from first cable needle.

Stitch Pattern
Cable Columns Pattern (19 sts)
Row 1 (RS): K1, p2, [k2, p2, k2, p1] twice, p2.
Row 2 (WS): P1, k2, [p2, k2, p2, k1] twice, k2.
Row 3: K1, p2, 1/1 RC, p2, [k2, p1] twice, p1, 1/1 RC, p3.
Row 4: P1, k2, [p2, k2, p2, k1] twice, k2.
Row 5: K1, p2, [k2, p2, k2, p1] twice, p2.
Row 6: P1, k2, [p2, k2, p2, k1] twice, k2.
Row 7: K1, p2, 1/1 RC, p2, 2/1/2 RPC, p2, 1/1 RC, p3.
Row 8: P1, k2, [p2, k2, p2, k1] twice, k2.
Rep Rows 1–8 for patt.

Cable Columns Pattern

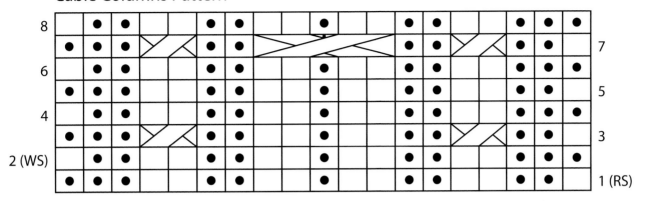

	RS: k; WS: p
•	RS: p; WS: k
	1/1 RC
	2/1/2 RPC

Scarf

CO 19 sts.
Work Cable Columns Patt until scarf measures approx
  60"/152 cm or to desired length, ending with Row 2.
BO in patt.

Finishing

Weave in ends.
Block to length.

Meherrin Scarf

Skill Level: **Easy**

Rustic and warm, knit and purl stitches work together to create a lofty basket-weave effect. This wonderfully squishy yarn is quick to knit—you'll have a cozy, soft scarf in no time at all!

Finished Measurements
Width: 6¾"/17 cm
Length: 62½"/158.5 cm, before fringe

Yarn
Lion Brand Wool-Ease Chunky, bulky weight #5 yarn (80% acrylic, 20% wool; 153 yd/5 oz, 140 m/100 g per skein) 3 balls #144 Eggplant

Needles and Other Materials
• US size 11 (8 mm) knitting needles or size needed to obtain gauge
• US J-10 (6 mm) crochet hook
• Tapestry needle

Finished Gauge
17 sts x 15 rows in Ladder Patt, stretched lengthwise heavily and blocked = 4"/10 cm
Save time by taking time to check gauge.

Note
• Cut the fringe pieces before you start so you can work the scarf until you have just enough yarn for the bind-off. Set them aside until you need them.

Stitch Pattern
Ladder Pattern (multiple of 6 sts + 5)
Row 1 (RS): Sl1, *k3, p1, k1, p1; rep from * to last 4 sts, k4.
Row 2 (WS): Sl1, p3, *k3, p3; rep from * to last st, k1.
Rows 3–6: Rep Rows 1–2 twice.
Row 7: Sl1, *p1, k1, p1, k3; rep from * to last 4 sts, [p1, k1] twice.
Row 8: Sl1, k3, *p3, k3; rep from * to last st, k1.
Rows 9–12: Rep Rows 7–8 twice.
Rep Rows 1–12 for patt.

Ladder Pattern

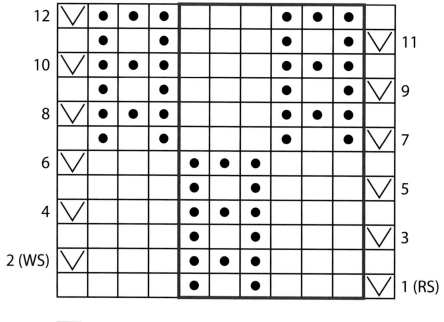

- ☐ RS: k; WS: p
- ● RS: p; WS: k
- ☒ RS: sl 1; WS: sl 1

Scarf

CO 29 sts.
Work Ladder Patt for a total of 19 repeats.
Rep Rows 1–6.
For a longer scarf, continue to work in patt until yarn
 is almost gone, leaving enough for bind-off.
BO on next RS row.

Finishing

Block to measurements.
Weave in ends.

Fringe

Cut 16 pieces of yarn 14"/35.5 cm long. Fold one strand
 in half and, starting at corner of scarf, with RS facing,
 insert crochet hook from back to front. Place the folded
 loop of the yarn over the hook and pull through to
 back. Like a yarn over, wrap the tails of the yarn over
 the hook and pull all the way through the loop on the
 hook, tightly. Repeat 7 more times, evenly spacing
 fringe across end of scarf.
Repeat with 8 remaining strands on other end of scarf.
 Trim as needed.

How to Use This Book

Every knitter needs a little guidance once in a while, so follow the tips, suggestions, and tricks in this section to ensure your success from cast-on to bind-off.

Yarn

You'll find the specific yarn recommended listed in the pattern, but sometimes that yarn may not be available or you'd like to try something different. To change it up, start by checking out the weight and the gauge for that yarn. Yarn weight refers to the thickness of the yarn, with the higher number indicating a heavier yarn. The Craft Yarn Council of America (CYCA) has a yarn classification system that simplifies the yarn-choosing process. You'll want to find a comparable yarn in the same weight indicated in the pattern. The weights used in this book are from the bulky #5 and super bulky #6 categories.

However, just because a yarn may be the same weight as the yarn called for in the pattern doesn't automatically mean it is suitable for the project. Your next step is to check out the fiber content. Different fibers have their own unique characteristics that affect everything from drape and gauge to comfort and style, so aim for a yarn that is as close in fiber content as possible to that of the original yarn. Once you've narrowed down your search, work a gauge swatch to ensure that your chosen yarn will work for the pattern.

Gauge

Gauge is one of the most critical aspects of knitting and refers to how many stitches or rows equal an inch *after* (and this is important) the piece has been washed and dried. For example: 20 sts x 30 rows in St st, blocked = 4"/10 cm.

When it comes to gauge, fabric that is hot-off-the-needles differs from fabric that has been blocked. While it isn't critical to match gauge on most accessory patterns, changes to your finished gauge will result in changes in the project size as well as the amount of yarn used, so

keep that in mind. Knitting garments, or anything you want to fit, is an entirely different matter! You'll need to work up a gauge swatch, or sample, of the stitch pattern to ensure your stitch count matches the pattern so that your final garment will also match the measurements given.

To work a gauge swatch, cast on the recommended number of stitches listed under "finished gauge" for 4"/10 cm with the suggested needle size in the stitch pattern indicated. Work 4"/10 cm in length and bind off loosely. Block your swatch according to the yarn care label (steam or wet-blocked depending on the fiber content; treat the fabric exactly as you would the finished product). After the swatch is dry, lay the swatch, public side facing down, on a flat surface. Measure the width from edge to edge. If the finished swatch is less than 4"/10 cm wide, you'll need larger needles and will likely need to swatch again until you get gauge. If wider than 4"/10 cm, you'll need smaller needles.

Sizing

Each pattern in this book indicates its finished measurements, whether bust circumference or length. The garments are geared to fit about 2 to 3"/5 to 7.5 cm larger than your actual bust circumference, while the hats are aimed at approximately 1"/2.5 cm smaller than your actual head circumference, so choose a finished measurement with that in mind. For a garment or hat, it also indicates the average size that the finished measurements correspond to, so feel free to utilize that instead.

Reading Charts

Some of the patterns in the book include a chart for you to refer to. While written instructions are always provided, it's good to stretch the brain and learn new skills!

Flat charts are read from right to left on right-side rows and left to right on wrong-side rows. It gets a little weird when reading wrong-side rows because you'll need to do the opposite of what the stitch symbol looks like. For example, a blank square indicates a knit on the right side, but on the wrong side, it would be a purl. The reason for this is so that the chart can be a visual representation of what the right side of your fabric looks like.

Circular charts are read from right to left on every row. Also, every stitch symbol is exactly what it says it is, i.e., a blank square means knit on every row it appears in.

Always consult the stitch key to understand what the symbols mean.

Example of a chart for a piece knitted back and forth in rows.

Wave Lace Pattern

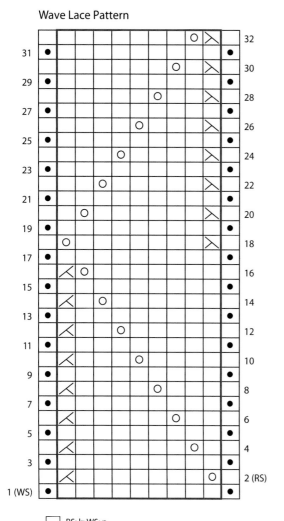

RS: k; WS: p
WS: k
yo
k2tog
ssk

Block to Measurements

"Block to measurements" means that you are going to wet or heat your project, which teaches all of the stitches how to hold hands and behave together, and then block, or shape and dry.

Steam Blocking

Steaming (my favorite method) is done quickly and easily, but it doesn't work for every fiber (avoid metallic and bamboo, for sure, as well as 100% nylon). Many acrylics, especially when blended with wool, can handle the rigors of steam blocking, but always test it on a small sample first.

1. Begin by pinning the edges out to the schematic or finished measurements and gently steam your piece. If you are using an iron, do not press it to the fabric—keep the steam about an inch above the fabric.
2. While the piece is still damp, use your fingers to pinch any cables or pull open any eyelets. I typically pin my edges down to smooth them out, which is especially helpful if they will be seamed together.
3. To block ribbing, pat the ribbed area to condense it, then allow the steam to permeate it. Let it dry and then give a few quick pulls widthwise, then a few quick pulls lengthwise. This really makes it fluffier and more pronounced.

Wet Blocking

Wet blocking isn't hard, but it can be time-consuming and a space hog. Wet blocking is necessary for most fine-gauge lace (lace weight), specialty yarns such as bamboo or cashmere, or for blooming certain wools.

1. Soak the pieces in a sink full of lukewarm or cool water. I often drop in a bit of no-rinse wool wash to help reduce some of the wooly odor or vinegar smell that hand-dyed yarns can initially have.
2. Lift the wet piece out without stretching, roll it up, and squeeze out the excess water. Then lay it on a towel, roll it up again, and step on the towel to remove the last bit of water.
3. Lay out your pieces on a safe surface, such as a mattress or blocking board, and pin to shape. If your piece has points or scallops, this is where you define them, pinning them out as much as necessary to hold them in shape.

Abbreviations

approx	approximately
beg	begin(ning)
BO	bind off
CO	cast on
dec(s)	decrease(s)
dpn(s)	double-pointed needles
est	establish(ed)
foll	following
inc(s)	increase(s)
k	knit
kfb	knit in front and back of stitch
kfbf	knit in front, back, and front of stitch
k2tog	knit 2 stitches together
k3tog	knit 3 stitches together
LH	left hand
m	marker
M1	make 1
p	purl
patt	pattern
pm	place marker
psso	pass slipped stitch over
p2tog	purl 2 stitches together
rem	remain(ing)
rep(s)	repeat(s)
RH	right hand
rnd(s)	round(s)
RS	right side
s2kp	sl 2 sts as if to knit, knit 1, pass slipped sts over
sk2p	sl 1 st as if to knit, k2tog, pass slipped st over
sl	slip
ssk	sl next st as if to knit, the next stitch as if to purl, then insert the LH needle into the front of both stitches and knit together through the back loop
st(s)	stitch(es)
St st	stockinette stitch
tbl	through the back loop(s)
tog	together
WS	wrong side
yo	yarn over

Stitches & Techniques

Whether you need a refresher or are ready to learn a new technique, the tutorials in this section provide step-by-step instructions and photographs that will make you a master knitter in no time at all.

Cable Cast-On

The cable cast-on is super handy for buttonholes and middle-of-the-row cast-ons because of its firm, smooth edge. It's pretty easy to work, too!

1. Insert the tip of the RH needle *between* the first and second stitches on the LH needle.

3. Place that loop onto the LH needle in front of the first stitch. You've now cast on one stitch.

2. Wrap your yarn around the right tip just as if you were knitting a regular stitch. Pull that loop through between the two stitches to the front.

4. Repeat Steps 1–3 until you have cast on all the stitches required.

Knit Front-Back (kfb) Increase

This stands for "knit into the front and back of the next stitch" and results in one increase (one stitch turns into two).

3. Before dropping that old stitch from the LH needle, take the tip of your RH needle and insert it into the back loop of the same stitch you just knit, wrap the RH needle as if to knit, and . . .

1. Knit into the next stitch like normal and . . .

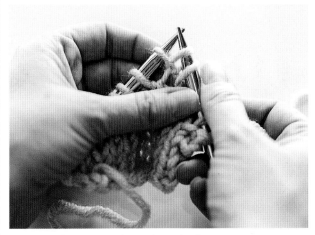

4. . . . pull your yarn through to the front.

2. . . . pull your new loop through to the front.

5. Now you can drop that old stitch from the LH needle. You've increased one stitch.

Knit Front-Back-Front (kfbf) Increase

This stands for "knit into the front and back and front of the next stitch" and results in two increases (one stitch turns into three).

3. Before dropping that old stitch from the LH needle, take the tip of your RH needle and insert it into the back loop of the same stitch you just knit, wrap the RH needle as if to knit, and . . .

1. Knit into the next stitch like normal and . . .

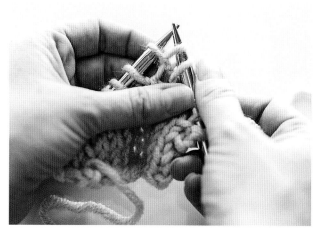

4. . . . pull your yarn through to the front.

2. . . . pull your new loop through to the front.

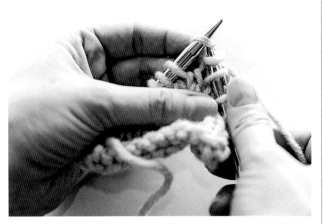

5. Still not dropping that old stitch from the LH needle, insert the RH needle tip back into the front of the same stitch you just knit, wrap the RH needle as if to knit, and pull your yarn through to the front.

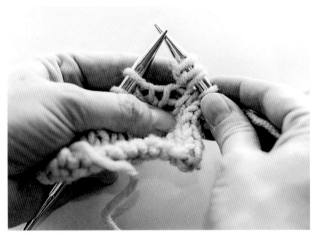

6. Now you can drop that old stitch from the LH needle. You've increased two stitches.

Make 1 (M1)

This increase adds a stitch by lifting the bar between the stitches and knitting into it. It's ideal because it helps maintain patterns a little bit better while being less noticeable than the kfb.

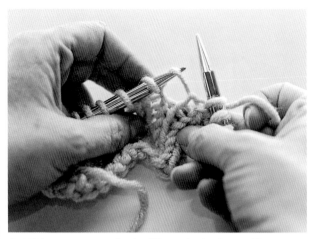

1. With your LH needle tip, lift up the horizontal bar between the stitches, from front to back.

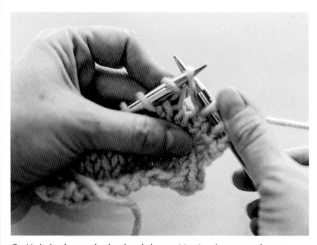

2. Knit it through the back loop. You've increased one stitch.

Slip 2, Knit 1, Psso (s2kp) Decrease

This two-stitch decrease results in a centered-looking stitch.

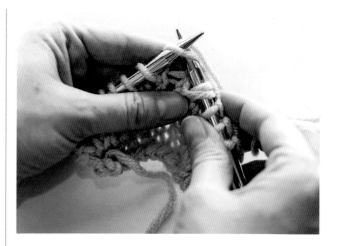

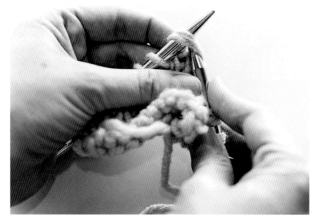

1. Insert your RH needle into the next 2 stitches as if to knit, but . . .

3. Knit the next stitch like normal.

2. . . . slip them over, together, unworked, to the RH needle.

4. Insert the tip of the LH needle into the slipped stitches and . . .

5. . . . lift them up and over the stitch just knit, right off the needle.

You've decreased two stitches.

Slip 1, Knit2tog, Psso (sk2p) Decrease

This two-stitch decrease is similar to the one-stitch decrease of slip 1, knit 1, psso.

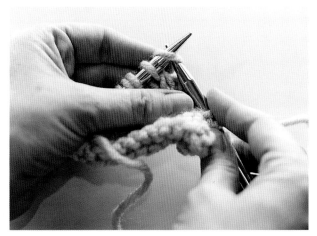

1. Insert your RH needle into the next stitch as if to knit, and . . .

2. . . . slip it over, unworked, to the RH needle.

(continued)

3. Knit the next two stitches together.

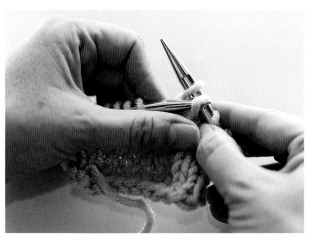

4. Insert the tip of the LH needle into the slipped stitch and lift it up and over the two stitches you knit together and off the RH needle.

You've decreased two stitches.

I-Cord

I-cord comes in handy for a variety of purposes, including belts, ties, trims, and straps. You'll need a set of double-pointed needles or a circular needle.

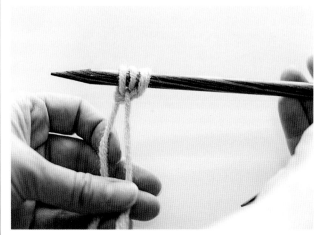

1. Cast on the required number of stitches onto a dpn or circular needle.

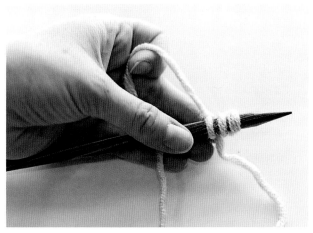

2. Instead of turning your work, keep the same side facing you and push the stitches to the other end of the needle.

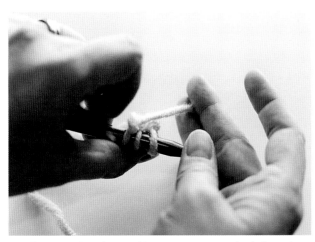

You'll notice that the working yarn stays to the left at the back.

3. Maintaining that set-up, knit across the stitches as normal. You'll want to give the yarn a good tug at first to bring it across the back of the knitting. Now, don't turn!

4. Instead, repeat Steps 2–3 until your I-cord is at its desired length.

3-Needle Bind-Off

The 3-needle bind-off is worked when two ends need to be joined together with live stitches. It's a good alternative to the more fiddly Kitchener stitch, but has the drawback of producing a seam. You'll need 3 needles to complete this bind-off.

1. With the RS facing each other, divide your stitches between two knitting needles. Hold the needles parallel to each other and just as if you were knitting with one.

2. Insert a third knitting needle into the first stitch on the first needle facing you as in a normal knit stitch.

(continued)

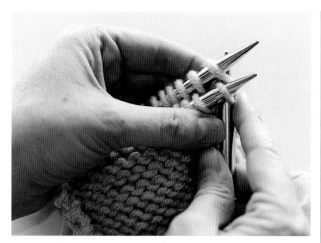

3. Insert the same needle as if to knit into the first stitch on the back knitting needle.

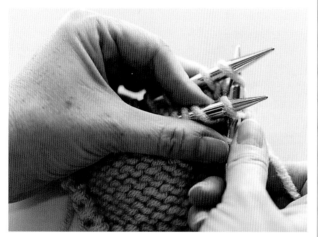

4. Knit both stitches together like normal, pulling your yarn through both stitches.

5. Knit the next two stitches, one from the front needle and one from the back needle, together in the same way. You now have two stitches on your RH needle.

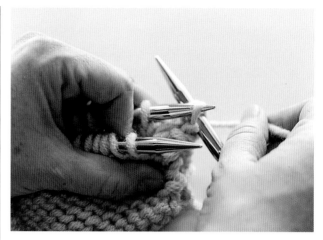

6. Bind off one stitch like normal, lifting the rightmost stitch on the RH needle over the left stitch and off the needle.

7. Repeat Steps 5–6 to bind off all stitches.

Kitchener Stitch

Kitchener stitch, or grafting, is worked when two ends with live stitches need to be joined together seamlessly and smoothly. You'll need two knitting needles and a tapestry needle.

1. Make sure your stitches are divided evenly between two needles and hold them parallel to each other with the RS facing out and WS facing in. Thread your tapestry needle with yarn twice the length of the piece you are seaming. Imagine your tapestry needle is like a knitting needle and insert it into the first stitch on the front needle as if to purl. Pull the yarn all the way through, leaving the stitch on the needle.

2. Next, insert the tapestry needle through the first stitch on the back needle as if to knit. Pull the yarn through, leaving the stitch on the needle and being careful that the yarn doesn't wrap around the front needle in the process.

3. Now, insert the tapestry needle through the first stitch on the front needle as if to knit.

4. Pull the yarn all the way through and drop the stitch off the front needle.

5. Insert the tapestry needle into the next stitch on the front needle as if to purl and pull the yarn through, leaving the stitch on the needle.

(continued)

6. Moving to the back needle, insert the tapestry needle into the first stitch as if to purl.

8. Insert the tapestry needle into the next stitch on the back needle as if to knit.

7. Pull the yarn all the way through and drop the stitch from the needle.

9. Repeat Steps 3–8 until all stitches have been worked.

Visual Index

**Monday
Moebius
Cowl**
page 1

**Apple River
Shrug**
page 4

**Hanalei
Wrap**
page 9

**Ashaway
Scarf**
page 12

**Marias
Cowl**
page 15

**Kachess
Hat**
page 19

**Abita
Pullover**
page 22

**Fresno
Braided
Headband**
page 27

**Sekiu
Hat**
page 29

**Calumet
Shawlette**
page 32

**Brandywine
Tunic**
page 36

**Isinglass
Capelet**
page 42

**East Twin
Bracelet Set**
page 44

Mazon Vest
page 46

**Lynnhaven
Cowl**
page 50

**Lynnhaven
Headband**
page 53

**Cahaba
Hat**
page 56

**Cahaba
Mitts**
page 59

**Saluda
Hood**
page 62

**Genessee
Vest**
page 64

**Baker
Slouch Hat**
page 69

**Mojave
Cowl**
page 73

Kenai Cowl
page 75

Byram Shawl
page 78

Blue Harbor Scarf
page 81

Meherrin Scarf
page 84